Guide to

Having
a Baby

The Simple Guide to
Having a Baby

Janet Whalley, RN, IBCLC

Penny Simkin, PT

Ann Keppler, RN, MN

of Parent Trust for Washington Children

Meadowbrook Press

Distributed by Simon & Schuster
New York

Library of Congress Cataloging-in-Publication Data

Whalley, Janet, 1945-
    The simple guide to having a baby : what you need to know /
by Janet Whalley, Penny Simkin, Ann Keppler.
        p. cm.
        Includes index.
        ISBN 13: 978-0-88166-482-9 (Meadowbrook)
        ISBN 13: 978-0-684-03129-3 (Simon & Schuster)
        1. Pregnancy. 2. Childbirth. 3. Infants (Newborn)—Care.
I. Simkin, Penny, 1938- II. Keppler, Ann, 1946- III. Title.
        RG525.W59 2005
        618.2—dc22
            2004029005

Editorial Director: Christine Zuchora-Walske
Editor: Joseph Gredler
Proofreader: Megan McGinnis
Production Manager: Paul Woods
Graphic Design Manager: Tamara Peterson
Cover Photo: © GettyImages
Index: Beverlee Day

The contents of this book have been reviewed and checked for accuracy and appropriateness
by medical doctors. However, the authors, editors, reviewers, and publisher disclaim all
responsibility arising from any adverse effects or results that occur or might occur as a
result of the inappropriate application of any of the information contained in this book.
If you have a question or concern about the appropriateness or application of the treatments
described in this book, consult your health care professional.

Published by Meadowbrook Press
                5451 Smetana Drive
                Minnetonka, MN 55343

www.meadowbrookpress.com

BOOK TRADE DISTRIBUTION by Simon and Schuster, a division of Simon and
Schuster, Inc., 1230 Avenue of the Americas, New York, New York 10020

15 14 13 12 11 10   10 9 8 7 6 5

Printed in the United States of America

Dedication

To the thousands of new and
expectant parents we've worked
with over the years

and

to our families, who have taught
us about birth and being parents.

Doug Whalley

Scott and Heidi Whalley, Mike Whalley,
Kristin Platt, and Brian Platt

Peter Simkin

Andy, Bess, Freddy, Charlie,
and Eva Rose Simkin

Linny Simkin and Jeff,
Peter, and Callie Jobson

Mary Simkin-Maass and Greg,
Sara Jane, and Amelia Maass

Elizabeth Simkin, Nick Boyar,
and Cole Simkin-Boyar

Jerry Keppler

Eric and Courtney Keppler,
and Heidi Keppler

Contents

Thank You

We wish to thank our editors: Joseph Gredler, Megan McGinnis, and Christine Zuchora-Walske.

We want to thank the following people, who read the book and gave us helpful comments and suggestions:

Janelle Durham, M.S.W., Education Director of Parent Trust for Washington Children

Katie Ladner, B.S., birth educator, nutritionist for Belfair Women, Infants, and Children (WIC) Program

Lauren Valk Lawson, R.N., M.N., public health nurse for Public Health—Seattle & King County

Creagh Miller, doula and birth educator for Spanish-speaking families

Tera Schreiber, J.D., former Executive Director of Great Starts Birth & Family Education (now a program of Parent Trust for Washington Children)

We wish to thank those who helped with the drawings and design of this book: Tamara Peterson, Susan Spellman, Ruth Ancheta, and Childbirth Graphics, Ltd.

We appreciate the help and support from the members, board of directors, and staff of Parent Trust for Washington Children, and its Great Starts program, which has been helping new families since 1956.

Introduction

We wrote *The Simple Guide to Having a Baby* to help you understand what happens during pregnancy, birth, and the weeks after having your baby. During these exciting experiences, you'll learn amazing things about yourself. And you'll discover the wonder of pregnancy, the power of labor, the joy of birth, and the rewards of parenthood.

With this book, we want to help you:

1. Have a healthy and comfortable pregnancy. We hope to make the months of waiting more enjoyable and less stressful.

2. Plan and prepare for childbirth. We hope you have a safe and satisfying birth experience.

3. Learn more about babies and being a new parent. We hope you'll feel more confident as a mother or father.

We hope this book helps answer many of your questions. If you want more information, please read our book *Pregnancy, Childbirth, and the Newborn: The Complete Guide*.

Wishing you a happy birth day and joyful parenting,

Janet Whalley, Penny Simkin, and Ann Keppler

Helpful Hints for Reading This Book

To understand new words or medical terms: Look in the index on pages 257–266. Page numbers in **bold** type show where you'll find the explanations of words or terms. Page numbers in regular type show where you'll find those words or terms on other pages.

To find more information on a topic within this book: When a topic is discussed in more than one section of the book, we include the other page numbers to help you find it (for example, "See pages 32–34").

To find more information outside this book: We've included a section called "Help and Resources for You and Your Baby" on pages 251–255. This section gives the names and contact information of agencies that provide helpful services for new parents.

CHAPTER I

Now That You're Pregnant

Pregnancy is a time of wonder. You wonder what you'll feel like later in your pregnancy. You wonder how your baby grows. You may also wonder about birth and how it'll feel to become a parent. This section describes what's happening during pregnancy, including:

- How your body changes shape

- The new feelings you'll have

- The amazing growth of your baby

✖ Jenny's Story ✖

I was shocked when I found out I was pregnant. I thought we were being careful. It took a while, but I finally got used to the idea. Kyle was mad at first. He said he wasn't ready to be a father. Pretty soon, we were excited about having a baby. All of a sudden, I started noticing cute babies everywhere. There are so many cute clothes and toys. I know it's hard to be a parent, but I think it'll be worth it. I already love my baby, and he or she isn't even born yet!

Being Pregnant

A woman can become pregnant by having sexual intercourse around the time her *ovary* (sex gland inside her belly) releases an egg. When a man's semen goes into her vagina, his *sperm cells* (from his sex glands called *testicles*) travel toward her egg. When one sperm cell enters her egg, she becomes pregnant. Look at the drawing of a woman before pregnancy (below) to see how your body looks inside.

When you're pregnant, you learn a lot of about having a baby. You also learn new things about your body and how it works. In this section, you'll probably find many new words. Knowing what they mean will help you understand what your doctor or midwife is talking about at visits during your pregnancy. Also, reading this book will be easier if you know a few medical words and terms.

- The unborn baby is called a *fetus*.

- The *placenta* makes *hormones* (substances that tell your body to make changes that are needed to grow a baby). These hormones (estrogen and

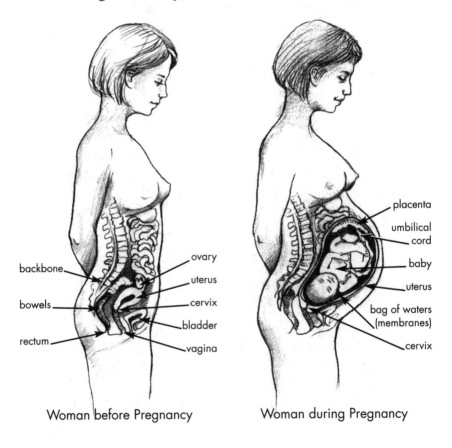

Woman before Pregnancy   Woman during Pregnancy

progesterone) affect how you feel both physically and emotionally.

- The *umbilical cord* connects the placenta to your baby. It carries food nutrients to your baby and takes away waste products.

- The *membranes* are filled with *amniotic fluid*. This is why the amniotic sac is also called the bag of waters. Your baby floats inside the bag of waters. The fluid protects your baby and allows her to move easily.

During pregnancy, your uterus is your baby's home.

- The *uterus* (sometimes called the *womb*) is a bag made of thick muscles. It's located in the pelvis behind the *bladder* (where *urine* or pee collects) and in front of the *rectum* (where your poop comes out). When you're not pregnant, your uterus is about the size of a pear. During pregnancy, it expands to hold your growing baby.

- The lower part of the uterus, called the *cervix*, leads into the vagina.

- During pregnancy, a *mucous plug* in the cervix closes the opening and protects the baby.

- The *vagina* is the birth canal. During birth, the vagina stretches to allow the delivery of the baby. After birth, it returns to its previous size.

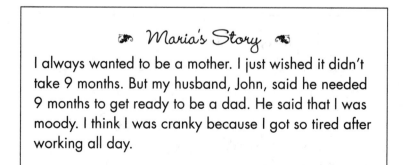

❧ Maria's Story ❧

I always wanted to be a mother. I just wished it didn't take 9 months. But my husband, John, said he needed 9 months to get ready to be a dad. He said that I was moody. I think I was cranky because I got so tired after working all day.

When Will Your Baby Be Born?

Your *due date* is a day close to the time your baby is ready to be born. It's only an estimate (best guess) of the birth date, but it's helpful to know. How did your doctor or midwife know your due date?

Pregnancy lasts about 40 weeks from the first day of your last menstrual period. To learn your due date, your caregiver wrote down the date of the first day of your last menstrual period. Then he or she subtracted 3 months from that date and added 7 days.

$$\begin{array}{r} \textit{(Date of first day of last period)} \\ - \textit{(3 months)} \\ + \textit{(7 days)} \\ \hline = \textit{(due date)} \end{array}$$

For example...

$$\begin{array}{r} \textit{(Last period started on)} \text{ July 10} \\ - \textit{(3 months)} \text{ April 10} \\ + \textit{(7 days)} \text{ April 17} \\ \hline = \textit{(due date)} \text{ April 17 of the next year} \end{array}$$

Some babies come early and some come late. Most babies are born within 10 days of their due dates. But babies don't usually come right on their due dates. So, expect your baby anytime from 2 weeks before to 2 weeks after your due date.

✲ Tanya's Story ✲

I had planned my second pregnancy so my daughter would be about 3 years old when the baby was born. I'd hoped that my mom could come and help me at home. Last time, she had to work and couldn't get away. This time, I tried to get pregnant so the baby would be born in the summer when she wasn't working at the grade school. Luckily, I got pregnant only a month after we started trying.

What Happens during Pregnancy?

During your pregnancy, you may feel different than you ever have before. You begin to see the physical changes in your body and you feel some emotional changes, too. Your baby also grows and changes rapidly.

Pregnancy is divided into 3 time periods (called *trimesters*) with each time period lasting about 3 months. Most people say that pregnancy lasts 9 months. Actually, it lasts a little longer (about 40 weeks total).

Changes in the First 3 Months of Pregnancy

This is the "forming" period for your baby. By the end of the first 3 months, all your baby's organ systems (such as the stomach, lungs, heart, and nerves) are formed and starting to work. By 14 weeks of pregnancy, your baby:

- Is about 3 inches long and weighs about 1 ounce
- Has eyes, ears, nose, and a mouth
- Makes breathing movements, but of course is not really breathing (Your baby gets oxygen from you through the umbilical cord.)
- Has arms with hands and fingers with fingerprints
- Has legs with knees, ankles, and toes
- Has a heartbeat that can be heard with a special stethoscope called a *Doppler*

During the first 3 months, your developing baby becomes quite active, although you probably don't feel any movements yet. His legs kick and his arms move. He can suck his thumb, swallow amniotic fluid, and *urinate* (pee) into the amniotic fluid. The fluid stays clean because it's refreshed or cleaned many times each day.

For you, the first 3 months of pregnancy is a time when your body and mind get used to being pregnant. In the beginning, you feel the effects of increased hormones. The physical changes include:

- No menstrual periods
- Nausea and vomiting (called "*morning sickness*," but may occur at any time during the day)
- Feeling tired and sleepy
- Frequent peeing
- More *discharge* (mucus) from your vagina (but not bad-smelling mucus)
- Changes in your breasts (which are already preparing for breastfeeding). Your breasts get bigger. Your nipples may tingle and feel tender. The area around each nipple (called the *areola*) gets darker.

The thought of being a mother may sometimes please you. But at other times you may worry and feel unhappy about being pregnant. You may cry easily. Finding out that you're pregnant can cause various emotions including:

- Mood swings (unexpected feelings of happiness or sadness)
- Happiness about having a cute little baby
- Sadness about having less freedom (needing to put the baby first all the time)
- Fear about how you and your partner might change
- Doubts about how good a parent you'll be
- Worry about not having enough money

By the end of the first 3 months, your uterus will be about the size of a grapefruit. Some women gain up to 5 pounds, but others do not. Although the physical and emotional changes may feel big to you, other people may not even notice that you're pregnant.

Changes in the Second 3 Months of Pregnancy

This is the "development" period for your baby. By 6 months of pregnancy, your baby is still tiny and not ready to be born. By the end of the 24th week, your baby:

- Is 11–14 inches long and weighs about 1½ pounds
- Has a strong heartbeat
- Begins to have fingernails and toenails
- Is able to suck her thumb
- Gets the hiccups
- Begins to hear
- Can roll around and move her arms and legs
- Has a strong grip

> ❧ *Maria's Story* ❧
>
> After 3 or 4 months, I had more energy. I got my
> appetite back, too. I started craving hot peppers. My
> friends thought it was funny. Sometimes peppers were
> all I wanted to eat! Nothing fit, so I wore John's shirts
> and left the top button of my jeans undone when I was
> at home. At work, I felt fat until I got some maternity
> clothes. The best part of all was when I started feeling
> our baby move! At first, it was a little fluttery feeling.
> Pretty soon, I knew it was our baby kicking and rolling
> around. She seemed strong and healthy.

You'll probably feel fine during these middle months
of pregnancy. Nausea usually goes away and you have
more energy. You might notice new signs of your growing
pregnancy, including:

- Your baby's movements (a light tapping feeling
  that may remind you of gas bubbles)

- Hard bowel movements (*constipation*)

- Food cravings

- Sharp pains in your lower belly or hip when
  you sneeze or stand up quickly

- A dark line (*linea nigra*) on your belly
  (abdomen) up to your bellybutton

- Darkening of the skin around your eyes and
  nose (called the *mask of pregnancy*), which
  usually goes away soon after the birth

- Stuffiness in your nose

- Bleeding from your gums or nose

- Weight gain (about 1 pound per week)
- Non-labor contractions of the uterus (*Braxton-Hicks contractions*). Some contractions are normal in pregnancy. When you have a contraction, your uterus tightens and your belly gets harder. You might be able to tell you're having Braxton-Hicks contractions if you notice your belly changing shape as your uterus presses against it. Or you might need to press on your belly with your fingers to feel if your uterus is hard. Sometimes contractions like these are a sign of having your baby too early (*preterm labor*). See page 27 to learn the difference between preterm labor contractions and Braxton-Hicks contractions.

At this time, your uterus is larger and you look pregnant. Some women enjoy how they look and feel, while others do not. You may:

- Think you're too fat, especially if you're having trouble moving around
- Feel more dependent on others
- Be more interested in babies and parenting
- Daydream and dream more at night
- Feel creative
- Notice changes in your feelings about sex

By the end of 6 months, your pregnancy seems more real to your family and friends. Now you look bigger. You can feel the baby move, and so can others when they touch your growing belly.

Changes in the Third 3 Months of Pregnancy

This is the "growth" period for your baby as she prepares for life outside your uterus. At the end of pregnancy, the baby's head is usually down. She kicks and wiggles, but doesn't turn and roll very much. She might get the hiccups. When she does, you'll feel her jerk just like you do when you have the hiccups. By the end of 40 weeks of pregnancy, your baby:

- Is about 20 inches long and weighs about 7–8 pounds
- Has fingernails that reach her fingertips
- Has more hair
- Has noticeable times of being awake and being asleep
- Hears sounds and voices

It's loud in the uterus. Your baby likes the sounds of your heart beating, your stomach gurgling, and the blood circulating through your placenta. You may notice that sudden, loud noises make her jump. Your baby can hear your voice. Try talking or singing to her.

❧ Tanya's Story ❧

I was surprised at how big I got in the last couple of months of this pregnancy. All of a sudden, I got some red stretch marks on my belly. That was upsetting. I'd hoped I wouldn't get them. It was August and I was hot all the time. I'd sit in the wading pool with my daughter. At night, I'd keep the fan pointed at me. I loved the baby moving. I called him Thumper. Jason called him Cool Max. I began thinking I couldn't wait till my due date. I wanted to meet our baby and stop feeling so fat and hot!

During the last 3 months of pregnancy, your uterus grows up to your ribs. Many of the common changes at this time come from having a bigger belly. You may notice some or all of these changes:

- It's hard to breathe deeply.
- You feel sore up by your ribs.
- The veins in your legs seem bigger.
- Your ankles swell.
- You have painful swelling of blood vessels in the rectum (*hemorrhoids*).
- Backaches bother you.
- You pee more frequently.
- Your sense of balance changes.

The hormones of pregnancy cause other changes including:

- Red *stretch marks* on your belly, thighs, or breasts (They fade to shiny lines after the birth.)
- Small red bumps or lines on your skin (*vascular spiders*)
- Feeling hot
- Trouble sleeping

Toward the end of pregnancy, your uterus tightens (contracts) more. These *prelabor contractions* help increase blood flow in your uterus. They also press your baby onto your cervix, making it softer and thinner. (See page 76 for more about how labor starts.)

About 2 weeks before the birth, your baby may drop lower in your pelvis. This is called *engagement* or *lightening*. You may find it easier to breathe and have less heartburn after your baby drops. However, you may need to go to the bathroom more as your baby's head presses on your bladder.

Expectant parents often have mixed feelings during this time in pregnancy. You may:

- Be ready for pregnancy to be over
- Need more help from others
- Worry about hurting your baby during sex
- Think more about your own parents and how they cared for you
- Have concerns about becoming a parent
- Be excited about having a new baby

All these feelings are normal. Talking about your fears and concerns with someone who's a good listener (your partner, a relative, your caregiver, or a friend) can help you feel better.

Near the end of pregnancy, you may think more and worry more about labor, birth, and the baby. By taking childbirth classes, you and your partner can learn more about labor, birth, and parenting. You worry less when you're prepared for these experiences.

Questions Asked during Pregnancy

Pregnant women have lots of questions. Depending on what's happening in your life when you're pregnant, you'll have certain questions and concerns. This section helps answer some of the questions you might have.

What about Sex during Pregnancy?

Your feelings about sex may change during pregnancy. These normal feelings are common:

- Some women may feel beautiful and sexual, while others may feel clumsy and fat.

- One woman may feel loved by a caring partner, while another may be alone or in a difficult relationship.

- One woman's partner may feel turned off by her growing belly, while another may love it.

- Some women don't want to have sex at all when they're pregnant; others do.

Body changes such as nausea, tiredness, or breast tenderness will affect your desire for sex. What you find exciting may also change. Some women don't want to have sex, but want to be hugged, cuddled, and loved. Your partner may or may not understand your changing interest in making love. Also, his sexual desires may change. Pregnancy can be stressful for both of you. Talk about your sex life. Try to understand and respect each other's feelings.

You should **not** have sexual intercourse if:

- Your caregiver told you not to have intercourse.

- You're at risk for preterm labor (labor occurring more than 3 weeks before your due date).

- You've had vaginal bleeding during pregnancy.

- You have painful cramps after intercourse.

- Your sexual partner has or might have a sexually transmitted disease (STD).
- You do not want to have sex.

Otherwise, it's okay to have sex. Though uterine contractions are normal when you have an orgasm, they don't cause problems for the baby during a healthy pregnancy. If you have a new partner during pregnancy, remember to use safe sex methods by having him use a condom. He might have a disease that may spread to you during sex (such as genital herpes, HIV, genital warts, or another infection).

Sex may be more comfortable if you don't lie on your back with your partner's weight on your belly. Try other positions such as lying on your sides with him behind you, or your partner on his back with you on top. If you don't want to have sexual intercourse, you can still cuddle.

Does Your Age Make a Difference?

Women can get pregnant anytime from their early teens to late forties. The best time seems to be between 20 and 35 years of age. Pregnancies have fewer problems at those ages. However, good health is more important than your age. Every woman should see a health caregiver as soon as she knows she's pregnant. At any age, good health care during pregnancy helps both you and your baby.

What about When You Already Have Another Child?

When you're pregnant again, it may not seem as exciting as your first pregnancy. You may wonder how your older child will react to the new baby. It may be harder to find time to rest. Also, going to doctor or midwife appointments may be more difficult when you have to take a child with you.

You may notice the pregnancy earlier. Pregnancy changes take place more easily in a body that's done it before.

- You feel the baby's movements earlier.

- Your uterus may get bigger sooner.

- You may notice more prelabor contractions toward the end of pregnancy.

Many second-time mothers worry about the next birth. "Will it be harder than last time?" "Will I be able to handle labor pain?" If a past birth experience was scary or if you had problems, you may worry about your next birth. These worries are normal. Talking about them with your partner and caregivers may help. If your caregivers know about your worries, they may be able to think of ways to help you feel better.

Many second-time mothers wonder if they have enough love for another child. You may feel that when you love your first child, the second will not get as much. Or you may worry that you'll love your first child less after the new baby arrives. These are common worries for many mothers. Remember that you can love many people. You don't run out of love. You can love another baby without taking love away from your older child.

❧ Tanya's Story ❧

I didn't enjoy pregnancy as much this time. Lifting my daughter and bending over to pick up toys made my back hurt. Jason and I didn't talk much about my pregnancy. We spent more time thinking about the new baby. We also wondered how Molly would like a brother or sister.

What If You're Expecting Twins, Triplets, or More?

When a woman is carrying more than 1 baby, it's called a *multiple pregnancy*. A sign of multiple pregnancy is hearing two or more heartbeats. Also you gain weight more quickly and your uterus grows faster than if you had 1 baby. An ultrasound scanner (a machine that uses sound waves to see inside you) shows that you're really having more than 1 baby.

Expecting multiples is exciting and stressful. Most people think twins and triplets are special, even though they're a lot more work. Growing more than 1 baby puts extra demands on your body. You may need to:

- Eat more food.
- Get more rest.
- Go to an *obstetrician* (a doctor with special training in treating childbirth problems) instead of a midwife or family doctor because the babies are often born too early.

If you're expecting multiples, you may want to talk to other parents who are expecting more than 1 baby. (For more information, see Parenting Resources on page 255.)

Is Pregnancy Different If You Have Been or Are Being Abused?

When someone has been physically, sexually, or emotionally abused, even long ago, it can cause unexpected reactions during pregnancy, birth, and *post partum* (after the birth).

Being hurt or abused by a more powerful person may make it hard to trust another powerful person. For example, you may not trust your doctor or midwife. A victim of sexual abuse may find vaginal exams or nakedness extremely upsetting. Some women who have been abused believe that the experience of having a vaginal birth would be unbearable.

If you've been abused in the past or if you're in an abusive relationship now, pregnancy and birth will be more stressful for you. Talk with your caregivers about your feelings and experiences. This may help you receive health care that's more sensitive to your needs.

No one deserves to be beaten, yelled at, or forced to have sex. If this is happening to you, you must protect yourself and your baby. Though you may feel like you can't get out of your situation, at least try to find places or people who can help you. They can also help you if you decide to leave. (See Pregnancy Health and Safety Resources on page 251 for ideas about where to go for support.)

Examples of Helpful People in a Support System

- Family and friends
- Nurses and staff at state and county health departments
- Church members and staff
- School counselors

What's It Like Being a Single Mother?

Pregnancy and parenthood may be difficult when you don't have a partner. Being a parent is hard work, and it's a job usually shared by 2 people. There may be times when you wonder if you can do it. You may feel lonely and wish you had a dependable partner. At other times, you may be thankful that you don't have to deal with a demanding or unkind partner.

It's especially difficult if you don't have family and friends to help you. This is a time to reach out to others for help and emotional support. (For more information about help for single mothers, see Parenting Resources on page 255.)

What about Being Pregnant When You Plan to Have Your Baby Adopted by Another Family?

When you're planning on adoption, you'll experience the feelings and changes of pregnancy, but the joy may not be there. This can be stressful. The weeks after the birth can also be difficult. Rely on your support system to help you cope with this challenging time.

The decision to give your baby to an adoptive family is one that many single women think about, especially if they're not ready or able to raise a child. It's not an easy decision for most women. You may go back and forth about it. It helps to talk it over with someone who isn't trying to make you decide either way. Talk with someone who will help you think about what's best for both the baby and you. Whatever you decide, you'll need kind people to support you. These people may also help you during the birth and afterward.

Some women go to childbirth classes to prepare for labor and birth. Even though you may feel uneasy in a class full of people who will keep their babies, you may find that you are well accepted and learn a lot about birth. Childbirth classes can improve your chances of having the best possible experience. You'll want to have good memories of your birth because you'll keep them for the rest of your life.

You may want to write a letter to the baby about the pregnancy and birth. Along with a baby toy or present, this could be a special gift from you.

A Special Note for Fathers

Waiting for your baby to be born can be exciting but difficult. It sometimes takes a while to get used to the idea of being a father, especially if the pregnancy was a surprise. As you start to think about your baby, you'll remember your own childhood—the good times and the tough times. You may remember some things that happened to you that you don't want your child to go through. Also, you may look forward to other things that you'll be doing together when your child is older.

A father-to-be sometimes thinks about all the changes that come with being a parent. You may worry about:

- *Losing your freedom.* You know that babies need constant care, and you'll be expected to help more around your home.

- *Having enough money.* You may feel like you're more responsible for supporting your family.

- *The possible death of your partner or baby.* This may lead you to be very protective of your partner. You may also worry about your own death.

- *Feeling unwanted.* You may feel that your pregnant partner doesn't love you as much as she did before she got pregnant. At the same time, you're expected to do more for her. It helps to talk to her about these feelings. She may not know how you're feeling.

- *Your role during labor and birth.* You may wonder, "What will I do during labor? Will I faint?" Childbirth classes, books, and talking with other fathers will help prepare you for your role during labor and birth. Also, having another person at the birth may take the pressure off you. (For more information about your role during labor, see page 121.)

- *Physical changes and discomforts.* Some men gain weight or have food cravings, nausea, or backaches—just like their pregnant partners. It's how you may show sympathy for your partner.

CHAPTER 2

Health Care during Pregnancy

While you're pregnant, you'll want to stay healthy. To do this, you need to have regular visits with a health caregiver who can check on you and your baby.

Prenatal Care Is Important

Prenatal care is the health care you get while you're pregnant. A doctor, midwife, nurse, or other health caregiver provides prenatal care. You'll have many appointments and some tests during your pregnancy. These help your caregiver:

- Check on your health
- Check on how well your baby is growing
- Find any problems and treat them before they become serious
- Show you how to care for yourself and your growing baby

At your first prenatal visit, you'll have a complete physical examination and several laboratory tests. You'll be asked about past illnesses and surgeries. Make sure your caregiver knows about any medications you're taking. You'll probably have time to talk about your concerns and plans for your pregnancy. During most of your pregnancy, you'll have appointments once a month. As you get closer to your due date, they'll be scheduled every 2 weeks or every week.

Sometimes it's hard to get to your appointments. If you have trouble getting to the office or clinic, or if the weather is bad, you may think about skipping one. Instead, try to find someone to take you. It's not a good idea to miss your checkups during pregnancy. You can ask a public health nurse about getting help with transportation or childcare. Your healthcare coverage may offer help, too.

To get the most from your visits, make a list of your questions and concerns before you go. If you do miss an appointment, call the office or clinic and schedule another time for a checkup.

If you have to take older children, time spent in the waiting room may seem to last forever. Bring toys for the children and a snack for all of you. Ask your partner or a friend to go with you.

✇ Jenny's Story ✇

I was thinking about skipping my appointment. It was too cold and wet outside to bother with the bus. My mother called to see how I was doing and found out I wasn't going. She got all upset and offered me a ride. I had to listen to her nagging all the way, but she was right. It was important to see my doctor. Now I know it's okay to call and ask for a ride.

What Are Your Choices for a Health Caregiver?

If you have health insurance, you need to find out what caregivers are available to you. If you have medical coupons, find out who takes them for maternity care. If you don't have insurance or coupons and can't afford to pay, check with your public health department or a social worker at a nearby hospital. You may be able to get help with prenatal care costs.

Caregivers for Pregnant Women

- *Obstetricians* are medical doctors who care for women during pregnancy and birth and for several weeks afterward.

- *Family doctors* provide medical care for the whole family. Some care for women during pregnancy, birth, and *post partum* (after the birth). They also see new babies.

- *Midwives* provide care for women who have a low risk of problems during pregnancy or birth. Most are certified nurse-midwives (CNMs) or state-licensed midwives (LMs).

- *Nurse practitioners* provide care in a clinic or office along with doctors or midwives. They see women before and after birth. They don't provide care for women during childbirth.

- *Naturopaths* are natural medicine doctors, not medical doctors. Some are also midwives and care for women during pregnancy, childbirth, and post partum.

Where Will Your Baby Be Born?

Most babies born in the United States and Canada are born in hospitals. You may or may not be able to choose your hospital. It depends on your healthcare coverage and where you live. To learn more about a specific hospital, take a hospital tour. Also, you may want to talk to friends about the different hospitals in your area. (For more on hospital tours, see page 68.)

Some women want to give birth at home or in an out-of-hospital birth center. Birth centers are smaller than hospitals and offer a homelike setting. Some women like them because there's less medical equipment.

The choice to have an out-of-hospital birth may be available in your area. However, you have this choice only if you have a *low-risk pregnancy* (one with no major problems) and expect a normal labor and birth. If there are problems during childbirth or you want pain medicine, you will be transferred to a hospital for care. The cost of an out-of-hospital birth is usually lower than the cost of hospital care. If you're interested in an out-of-hospital birth, check your health insurance or your local health department to see if the costs are covered.

What Prenatal Tests Are Usually Done?

During pregnancy, you'll have tests to find out how you and your baby are doing. To understand why a test is done, ask these questions:

- What's the purpose of the test?
- How is it done?
- Are there risks for my unborn baby or me?

You have the right to ask questions whenever you need more information to help you make the best choice about your care.

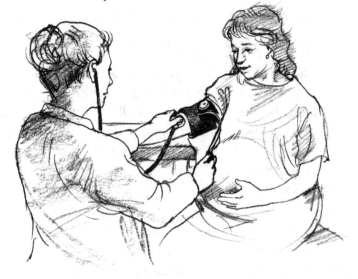

Common tests during pregnancy include:

- Urine tests
- Blood tests
- Blood pressure checks
- Weight checks
- Pelvic exams (Your caregiver checks for changes in your cervix by placing 2 fingers in your vagina.)
- Abdominal exams (Your caregiver feels your belly to check on your baby's growth and position.)
- Listening to your baby's heartbeat (*fetal heart rate or FHR*)

If one of those tests shows a possible problem, then other more specific tests may be ordered. Tests that look for these problems include:

- *Ultrasound scan* (Sound waves are used to create a video image of the uterus and baby.)
- *Amniocentesis* (Fluid from the uterus is withdrawn and tested.)
- Vaginal fluid collection and testing
- *Non-stress test* (Your caregiver listens to how the baby's heart rate responds when the baby moves within the uterus.)
- Other blood tests that show more than the first blood test

Warning Signs of Pregnancy Problems

If you notice any of the following, call your doctor or midwife right away:

- Bleeding from your vagina (even a small amount)
- Belly pain
- Tightening (contractions) or cramping in your belly that comes and goes (and continues for 1 hour or longer)
- Constant, painful tightness in your belly (with or without vaginal bleeding)
- Leaking or a gush of water from your vagina
- One or all of these signs of high blood pressure:
  - * Sudden swelling or puffiness in your hands, feet, or face
  - * Severe headache that lasts for hours
  - * Eyesight problems (spots, flashes, blurring)
  - * Severe dizziness, lightheadedness, or feeling faint
- Painful, red area on your leg (or pain in your leg when standing or walking)
- Pain or burning sensation while peeing
- Soreness, itching, or bad smell in your vagina
- Fever (a temperature of 100.4°F or 38°C or higher taken with a thermometer in your mouth)
- Nausea and vomiting that you can't stop by yourself
- No movement by your baby for 12–24 hours

When Should You Call Your Doctor or Midwife?

It's important to pay attention to how you feel during pregnancy. If you're worried or feel sick, call your caregiver. Also, if you have any warning signs of a pregnancy problem, call right away. Most problems can be treated before they become serious.

Possible Pregnancy Problems

Some of these problems might cause the warning signs listed in the box on page 26.

Preterm Labor

If you have contractions before the 37th week of pregnancy, you may be in *preterm labor*. Babies who are born too early have more health problems than babies born on time. For this reason, it's important to prevent or stop preterm labor contractions.

How Do You Know If You're Having Preterm Labor?

It's not easy to tell if you're having preterm contractions. Signs of preterm labor are very similar to normal sensations in pregnancy. Your caregiver can help you decide. Call your caregiver if you have two or more of these symptoms:

- Uterine contractions that are frequent and regular (more than 5 per hour that keep coming for 2 hours or more)
- Cramps causing discomfort in your lower belly
- Low, dull backache that's not from hurting your back
- Pressure in your lower belly or thighs (pelvic heaviness)

- More bowel movements (BMs) than usual or diarrhea

- Sudden increase or change in vaginal discharge (more mucus, water, or mucus with blood)

- General feeling that something isn't right

Checking for Contractions

Contractions come in waves as the uterus tightens and relaxes. When your uterus contracts, it feels hard. When it relaxes, it feels softer. Preterm contractions may not be painful. When contractions are constant and fairly regular and occur with some of the other symptoms listed on page 27 and above, you may be in labor. To check for contractions:

1. Drink 2 big glasses of water and then go pee.

2. Sit with your feet up and relax.

3. Place your fingertips gently but firmly on your belly at the top of your uterus to tell if the hardness occurs on a regular basis.

4. Count the contractions for 1 hour.

Call your doctor or midwife if:

- You're having contractions every 10 minutes or less. (This means 6 or more contractions in an hour.)

  and

- You've had other symptoms of preterm labor.

How Can You Stop Preterm Contractions?

Your caregiver may ask you to do these things to try to stop contractions and prevent a premature birth:

1. Drink plenty of water. Try to drink at least 8 glasses every day. Sometimes dehydration (not drinking enough water) causes contractions.

2. Stay in bed or spend less time on your feet.

3. Check for contractions and watch for other symptoms of labor.

4. Don't have sex.

5. Don't stroke or rub your nipples.

6. Take medications that your doctor or midwife gives you. Some drugs may stop labor. Others treat the cause (such as a bladder infection or vaginal infection).

✖ *Cami's Story* ✖

One day, I had to go to the bathroom all the time. Sometimes I almost didn't get there in time. And it burned when I peed. I knew something was wrong, so I called the doctor. He said that I probably had a bladder infection, and he ordered antibiotic pills. He said he was glad I'd called. If I'd waited, labor might have started and the baby would have been born too early. I'm glad I called him, too.

Infections

Certain infections during pregnancy may cause problems for you or your baby. Whether it's serious for the baby depends on when you get the infection and what it is. Some infections harm the baby only if you have them in the first 3 months (for example, German measles). Others are

---

dangerous if you have the infection when the baby is born (for example, genital herpes). In addition, some can cause problems at any time during pregnancy (for example, HIV). However, just because you get an infection doesn't mean your baby has been infected or harmed.

Make sure to tell your caregiver if you have any signs of an infection, such as:

- Fever
- Sores around your vagina
- Unusual vaginal discharge
- Pain when peeing
- Rash
- Vomiting
- Feeling sick

When you see your caregiver, you can be tested and treated, if necessary. Treatment for an infection depends on the type of germ (bacteria or virus) that's causing it. If bacteria are causing your infection, you'll probably get an *antibiotic* (a germ-fighting drug).

Diabetes

Diabetes means that you have a problem with too much sugar in your blood. It's because you have a problem making *insulin*, a hormone that helps your body use *glucose* (sugar) for energy. *Gestational diabetes* is a type of diabetes that starts during pregnancy. About the 26th week of pregnancy, most caregivers use a blood glucose test to find out if a woman has gestational diabetes.

Whether you have diabetes before pregnancy or get it during pregnancy, you'll need to take special care to control your blood sugar levels. This will help prevent problems for your baby, such as being too big, having low blood sugar, or developing birth defects. Treatment usually involves a special diet, regular exercise, and in some cases insulin shots.

High Blood Pressure

In pregnancy, high blood pressure (*hypertension*) can cause serious problems for you and your baby. *Pregnancy-induced hypertension* (PIH) is a type of high blood pressure that starts in pregnancy. PIH is sometimes called *preeclampsia* or *toxemia*. PIH makes it so that not enough blood gets to the uterus, which means less oxygen and nourishment for the baby. If not treated, PIH may get worse and cause seizures, coma, or even death of the mother.

Because it's important to find out if you have PIH, your blood pressure is taken at every prenatal visit. Finding out that you have high blood pressure early allows your caregiver to treat it so it doesn't become dangerous. Once your baby is born, your blood pressure usually returns to normal.

What Are the Symptoms of PIH?

You might have some of the following signs or symptoms. If you notice any of them, call your caregiver as soon as possible:

- Swelling (*edema*) especially in your hands and face
- Rapid weight gain
- Headaches, blurred vision, spots before your eyes
- Pain in your upper belly near your stomach

At your prenatal visits, your caregivers check for other signs of PIH by watching for:

- Blood pressure over 140/90 (mild PIH) or above 160/110 (severe PIH)
- Protein in your urine

How Can You Control High Blood Pressure?

If you have PIH, treatment depends on how serious it is. You may need to lie down more only during the day. Resting more and reducing stress in your life may be helpful. Also, try relaxing while lying down and using the slow breathing described on pages 116–117.

You may need to be on complete bed rest (staying in bed except to go to the bathroom or eat meals.) Staying in bed all the time is difficult, especially if you have toddlers at home. Try to get someone to help care for the children. And tell your caregiver if you'll have trouble following the directions to stay in bed.

You may get medicine to help lower your blood pressure or prevent harmful effects. It's important that you follow your caregiver's advice. Both you and your baby will be healthier.

Problems with the Placenta

In *placenta previa*, the placenta lies over the cervix. An ultrasound scan during pregnancy alerts your caregiver that you might have this rare condition. Often, a placenta that covers all or part of the cervix in early pregnancy moves away from the cervix and causes no problems later. But if the placenta stays over the cervix, a cesarean birth is planned before labor begins. (See pages 152–164 for more information on cesarean birth.) Sometimes placenta previa causes vaginal bleeding in the last month of pregnancy. This is not painful. However, you should call your doctor right away because it's a sign that your cervix is beginning to open.

With a *placental abruption*, the placenta begins to pull away from the uterus. This is rare, but if it happens, it occurs in the last months of pregnancy or during labor. If you have a placental abruption, you might have these symptoms: vaginal bleeding, severe abdominal pain, and hardness of the uterus. Your caregiver can tell the amount of separation by looking at an ultrasound scan. Treatment may be bed rest if the separation is small. If the baby is in danger, a cesarean birth is done.

Conclusion

After reading this section, it may seem like every pregnant woman has problems. In fact, most women have healthy pregnancies. With information about how to take care of yourself during pregnancy, you're likely to have a very healthy baby.

CHAPTER 3

Staying Healthy during Pregnancy

What you do (and don't do) during pregnancy can help you and your baby stay healthy. Pregnancy can also be a time to improve your health. By creating a healthier lifestyle now, you're more likely to continue it after your baby is born. This chapter tells how to be healthy, safe, and comfortable during pregnancy.

Tips for Having a Healthy Baby

1. Have regular prenatal care appointments.
2. Don't smoke, drink alcohol, or take street drugs.
3. Take your prenatal vitamin each day.
4. Follow your caregiver's advice about taking medicines.
5. Try to stay away from toxic chemicals and harmful situations.
6. Keep a healthy lifestyle by:
   - Eating healthy foods
   - Exercising regularly
   - Reducing stress
   - Getting enough sleep and rest
   - Wearing a seat belt

Eat Well during Pregnancy

Eating good foods is important for staying healthy and growing a healthy baby. During pregnancy, your unborn baby gets nutrients from the foods you've eaten. Also, your body stores nutrients in preparation for breastfeeding.

What Are Nutrients?

Nutrients include proteins, carbohydrates, fats, vitamins, minerals, and water. They come from food, pills, and food supplements, but eating food is usually the best way to get them.

Follow these guidelines to keep healthy during pregnancy:

- Eat a well-balanced diet.
- Gain the right amount of weight (not too little, not too much), around 20–35 pounds.
- Drink plenty of liquids each day.
- Take a daily prenatal vitamin pill that includes iron and folic acid.

Food Tip

To get enough vitamins and minerals, eat many different colored fruits and vegetables. Look for a variety of colors at the market or grocery store. Brighter or darker ones are best. For example, dark green lettuce is more nutritious than light green lettuce.

What Should You Eat?

During the last half of pregnancy, you'll need more healthy food than you did before pregnancy. This means eating a few extra servings each day. Eat a variety of foods, and focus on ones that are high in protein, calcium, and iron. Stay away from foods that aren't healthy, such as chips, cake, cookies, candy, and soft drinks.

Examples of Serving Sizes	
Vegetables	½ cup
Fruits	1 piece of fruit
Grains	1 slice of bread, 1 bagel, or ½ cup of cereal or uncooked rice
Dairy products	1 cup of milk or yogurt, or 1-inch cube of cheese
Protein foods	2 ounces of meat, poultry, or fish; 2 eggs; or ⅔ cup of nuts or cooked beans
Liquids	8 ounces of water or juice

A good daily pregnancy diet is one that includes plenty of the following foods:

- Fresh vegetables (4 servings)

- Fruits (3 servings)

- Whole-grain cereal and breads, tortillas, or rice (9 servings)

- Dairy products that provide calcium: milk, cheese, or yogurt (3 servings)

- Protein foods: meat, poultry, fish, nuts, eggs, or beans (3 servings)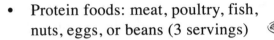

- Liquids: water (8 glasses) along with milk or juice

Some foods are especially important for pregnant women. Try to eat some of these types of foods each day:

- Iron-rich foods: red meats (beef, pork), dark meats (turkey, chicken), and egg yolks

- Foods with some iron: prunes, beans, lentils, almonds, walnuts, dark green vegetables, or blackstrap molasses

- A small amount of fat for cooking or adding flavor: oil (olive, canola, or vegetable) or butter

If you need help with your diet, contact your state agency of the Women, Infants, and Children (WIC) program. You can find your state's toll-free number by visiting www.fns.usda.gov/wic. If you're pregnant and your income is below a certain level, WIC supplies some healthy food.

What Should You Be Careful about Eating?

Caffeine. Coffee, tea, colas, and some other soft drinks contain caffeine. Some over-the-counter drugs for headaches and colds have caffeine, too. Read the labels to learn the ingredients. Also, chocolate has a chemical that's similar to caffeine.

There are problems with taking too much caffeine in pregnancy. Caffeine can change your baby's heart rate, just like it may affect yours. It also reduces calcium and water in your body. In addition, caffeine increases stress hormones, which cause blood vessels to get smaller. This may decrease oxygen and nutrients for your baby. To reduce your chances of having these problems, try to limit the number of caffeine drinks to 1–2 cups a day during pregnancy.

Herbs and supplements. Many herbal products and food *supplements* (anything added to your regular diet, including vitamins and minerals) are now available in drugstores. Some are helpful, but others may be harmful. The word *natural* does not always mean "safe." Because there isn't much known about the risks of most herbs, avoid taking them while pregnant unless you talk to your caregiver first.

Non-food substances. Food cravings are common in pregnancy and aren't harmful. Many women crave pickles, ice cream, and spicy foods. However, some women want to eat non-foods that might not be safe. They crave things like dirt, clay, ice, freezer frost, burnt matches, cigarette ashes, charcoal, and mothballs.

Craving non-food substances is called *pica*. Eating these things isn't good for you or your baby. They may replace important nutrients or be dangerous for your baby. If you have an urge to eat non-foods, talk to your caregiver. He or she can help.

Harmful germs and chemicals in foods. Check with your caregiver to learn what specific foods you should limit or avoid eating during pregnancy.

During pregnancy, you shouldn't eat foods that might carry germs that are dangerous for your baby. For example, you should avoid eating raw fish and shellfish and undercooked meats or luncheon meats. Look for the word *pasteurized* (cooked) on cheese labels, and avoid cheeses (such as blue cheese or Brie) that aren't pasteurized.

Some fish, such as shark and swordfish, should not be eaten at all in pregnancy. They contain large amounts of mercury, which is dangerous to unborn babies and children. Other fish, such as albacore tuna fish, have smaller amounts of mercury and can be eaten about once a week. Canned light tuna, salmon, shrimp, and catfish are low in mercury. They can be eaten about twice a week.

How Much Weight Should You Gain during Pregnancy?

By gaining 20–35 pounds, you're more likely to have a healthy baby than if you gain a lot more or a lot less. However, if you eat well and exercise, you can trust that the amount of weight you gain will be the right amount for you.

Weight gain is usually slow in early pregnancy. It's common to gain about 2–4 pounds in the first 3 months. Later in pregnancy, you'll gain about 1 pound a week. If you gain 27 pounds, you might wonder where the weight goes:

- Baby (7½ lbs.)
- Placenta, amniotic fluid, and bigger uterine muscle (5 lbs.)
- Extra blood and body fluid (8½ lbs.)
- Bigger breasts (1 lb.)
- Extra fat (5 lbs.)

This weight gain during pregnancy is normal and very healthy. Some of the weight (especially from fat) is needed to breastfeed your baby. After the birth, you gradually lose weight as you make breast milk.

Exercise to Stay Healthy

It feels good to stay active during pregnancy. As you get bigger, exercise helps improve your breathing and the flow of your blood. Exercise also helps with back pain.

What exercise is best for you? That depends on your health during pregnancy. Having a bigger belly makes it harder to move around. As your baby grows, you may become tired sooner. Check with your doctor or midwife if you have questions about exercise.

What kind of exercise should you do? *Low-impact exercise* is easier on your joints. This means no jumping or bouncing. Also, wear shoes that are made for walking or exercising. Good exercises include walking quickly, bike riding, swimming, and other low-impact exercises in or out of water. Also, many women enjoy yoga during pregnancy.

❧ Cami's Story ❧

In the first months of pregnancy, I went for a run several times a week. As my belly got bigger, it was hard to run as much. So, I switched to taking a fast walk in the park. In the last month, my walks got slower. Then, when my legs started swelling, I went to the community pool. Swimming was great. I was able to exercise and my feet were less swollen, too. My doctor said swimming was good for me.

Sports

Pregnancy is not a good time to start a new sport that requires good balance. If you're already playing a sport, you may keep doing it as long as you feel comfortable. However, try to avoid making sudden, jerking movements because pregnancy hormones increase the risk of hurting your joints.

Guidelines for Safe Exercise

To avoid injury and get the most benefit:

- Exercise 3 or 4 times a week.

- Don't hold your breath while exercising.

- Drink plenty of water and eat enough calories.

- Avoid strain and exhaustion. (Can you pass the talk test?)

- Stop if you feel pain or have a headache, nausea, trouble breathing, dizziness, vaginal bleeding, or strong uterine contractions.

- Avoid getting overheated. Don't exercise in hot, humid weather or when you're ill or have a fever.

Aerobic Exercise

Aerobic exercise speeds up your heart rate and makes you breathe faster. If you begin an aerobic exercise program, start slowly and gently. Avoid exhausting exercises. You can check how hard you're exercising by using the "talk test." If you're gasping and can't keep talking, then you're exercising too hard. Slow down until you're able to talk comfortably. Also, stop exercising if you have any pain.

A good aerobic exercise program for pregnant women includes:

1. At least 5 minutes of warm-up (slow, smooth movements and stretching)

2. About 15 minutes of vigorous aerobic exercise

3. At least 5 minutes of cool-down (mild activity while your heart rate returns to normal)

Exercising the Pelvic Floor Muscles

The *pelvic floor* (or *perineal*) muscles surround your vagina. They support your uterus and other organs. During pregnancy, these muscles may sag and become weaker. You may pee a little in your pants when you cough, sneeze, or laugh. You may continue to leak urine after your baby is born. Pelvic floor exercises (called *Kegels*) help prevent and treat this problem. Keeping your pelvic floor muscles in good shape will help prevent leaking throughout your whole life.

Pelvic floor exercises also help reduce swelling and the heavy feeling around your vagina. In addition, pelvic floor exercises may improve sex for you and your partner.

To check the strength of your pelvic floor muscles, try stopping the flow of urine while you're peeing. If you can't stop the flow, it's a sign of weak muscles.

Kegel Exercise (Pelvic Floor Contraction)

1. Get in any position (sitting, standing, or lying down).

2. Focus on the muscles around your *urethra* (where pee comes out) and vagina, *not* the muscles of your buttocks, thighs, or abdomen.

3. Tighten (contract) the pelvic floor muscles as you would to stop the flow of pee. It should feel like you're lifting the pelvic floor.

4. Hold the contraction as tightly as you can for a slow count of 10. (Don't hold your breath.) As your muscles get stronger, try holding for a slow count of 20.

5. Repeat 10 times throughout the day. (For example, do 1 or 2 while washing your hands or taking a shower.)

Have a Healthy Lifestyle

What else can you do to make your pregnancy as healthy as possible?

Get Enough Sleep and Rest

The amount of sleep you need may change as your pregnancy progresses. In early pregnancy, you may be sleepier than usual because of changes in your hormones. During the middle months, you may not need as much sleep. Later, as your baby grows, you'll use more energy to move around and you'll be tired again.

In late pregnancy, you'll probably wake up often during the night. So, try to sleep about 7–9 hours each night. This may mean that you have to go to bed earlier or stay in bed later to get that much sleep. When you're tired during the day, try to take a nap or sit down to rest. Even 10–20 minutes of rest during your coffee break or lunch break will help you feel better. Walking or being physically active during the day usually helps you sleep better at night.

Relax to Reduce Stress

When you're upset or things feel really crazy, take some time for yourself. Relax your tight muscles. You'll probably feel less stressed. Relaxation helps calm your mind and reduces muscle tension.

The first step in learning how to relax is paying attention to how your mind and body feel when you're falling asleep. Try to feel like this when you're relaxing. When you're drowsy, your breathing is slow and even. This type of breathing helps you anytime you're stressed. It also works during labor.

The next step is becoming aware of *muscle tension* (a tight feeling in your muscles). Try the Learning to Relax exercise on page 45 to help you do this.

Learning to Relax

When learning to recognize muscle tension, practice in a quiet, calm place.

1. Sit in a chair or on the floor.

2. Make a tight fist with your right hand. Pay attention to how your arm and hand feel. Touch the muscles in your forearm with your other hand. Muscles are hard when they're tense.

3. Open your right hand and relax it. Notice how soft the muscles feel when you release the tension.

4. Next, raise your shoulders toward your ears. Notice how you feel when your shoulders are tense.

5. Lower your shoulders and relax. Release even more. Now really relax. Did you notice how you released more muscle tension when you became aware of it?

6. Sometimes when you're stressed, your muscles tighten without your noticing. When you think about it, you realize how tense you are. At these times, relax and let go of that muscle tension.

Improve Stressful Relationships

Everyone has stressful relationships in some part of his or her life—with family, friends, or people at work. Most relationships have ups and downs. Pregnancy is a time to build strong and supportive connections with others.

Every pregnant woman needs someone in her life who cares for her and wants to help her. She needs someone she trusts and can talk to. Your partner, a family member, or a friend may be this person. If not, think of ways to work on your relationships so you have the support you need during pregnancy.

It may also help to meet other pregnant women by taking classes (prenatal exercise, yoga, or childbirth education) or by attending a pregnancy support group. Ask your caregiver about this. A social worker at the hospital may also help you find support groups.

✎ Jenny's Story ✎

I remember when my sister, Luann, was pregnant. She had to move home because her boyfriend was so mean to her. We were afraid that he'd hurt her when he was drunk. Mom had to kick my dad out when he was hitting her. She sure wasn't going to let Luann go through that, too. Mom helped Luann talk to the nurse about being abused. The nurse was real nice and told Luann where to go for help to keep her boyfriend away from her.

Getting Help from Others

What can your partner, family members, and friends do to help you during pregnancy?

- Provide a peaceful, safe home (without fighting, hitting, pushing, or yelling)

- Learn about pregnancy and how to help you during labor

- Help you eat a healthy diet and avoid harmful behavior

- Offer to help with household chores when you're tired

- Enjoy having fun with you (seeing a movie, taking a walk, having a heart-to-heart talk, or laughing together)

Buckle Up: A Healthy Habit

You and your unborn baby are safer when you wear your seat belt. In a car, use the shoulder and lap belts. This is safest and most comfortable. Keep the belts tight across your shoulders and low on your hips. Put the lap belt below the bulge of your belly. In an airplane, buckle the belt below the bulge of your belly like you would in a car.

Follow Your Caregiver's Suggestions about Taking Medicines

Don't take medicines during pregnancy unless you talk to your doctor or midwife first. Also, if your caregiver orders a medicine, make sure to take it.

Some medicines (such as antibiotics, insulin, and drugs for depression) treat an illness. Others only relieve symptoms such as pain, headache, runny nose, or cough. The medicines that treat an illness are more important to take than the ones that relieve symptoms.

When thinking about using medicines that make you feel better (but don't treat an illness), think about harmful side effects. Ask your doctor or midwife about them. If your caregiver says you can safely take a medicine, then use it. Otherwise, look for other ways to deal with your pain or discomfort, such as using the home remedies suggested below and on page 49.

A few common medicines that are harmless when you're not pregnant may cause problems when you're expecting a baby. Here's information about some of these.

Drugs that reduce pain or fever. Some pain relievers (such as aspirin, ibuprofen, and naproxen) increase the risk of bleeding in the mother and newborn baby. They also interfere with the start of labor. So, don't take them when you're pregnant. Acetaminophen (Tylenol) may be used in pregnancy, but take only the suggested dose. Too much Tylenol can harm you and your baby.

Home Remedies for a Headache

Instead of using medicine for a headache, try a warm bath, a massage, or tension-reducing exercises. Use the relaxation techniques suggested on pages 44–45. Hot packs or cold packs on the back of your neck or shoulders may feel soothing. Cold packs on your forehead may also help. Try to get more sleep, and find time to rest during the day. Hunger can cause headaches, so don't miss a meal. Also, drink plenty of water.

Drugs to relieve symptoms of a cold. Some of these medicines may be taken in pregnancy, while others should be avoided. Before you take any medicine for a cold, talk with your caregiver. Since some cold medicines have several ingredients, always read the labels. You'll want to take only the specific drugs suggested by your caregiver.

Home Remedies for a Cold, Runny Nose, or Cough

These measures are safe in pregnancy:

- Cool-mist vaporizer
- Saline nose spray or drops
- Sleep and rest
- Plenty of liquids
- Gargling with a mixture of honey and warm water

Drugs to treat nausea and vomiting. There aren't many safe drugs to help with vomiting during pregnancy. Talk to your caregiver to learn about any safe ones. Otherwise, try the suggestions on page 54 for reducing nausea and vomiting.

Avoid Possible Harmful Substances

Everything you eat, drink, or breathe affects you. Some things can be harmful for your baby, while others are not. Talk to your caregiver about what to avoid. Here are some warnings about substances that are harmful to unborn babies.

No Alcohol

Alcohol is very bad for your baby. When you drink, so does your baby. If you drink heavily during pregnancy, your baby may not grow or learn normally because of brain damage. Heavy drinking means 6 beers, 6 glasses of wine, or 6 shots of hard liquor each day. However, any amount of alcohol could harm your baby.

Even 3 drinks per day or getting drunk once during early pregnancy may cause mild learning and behavior problems for your child. Stop drinking when you're pregnant—the earlier the better. Instead of alcohol, drink fruit juice, vegetable juice, or sparkling water.

❧ Tanya's Story ❧

At a party, I saw a pregnant woman having a drink. She made me think about Bonnie's little boy at preschool. He acts funny and he's a slow learner. Bonnie told me that she drank a lot when she was expecting him. She didn't know it could hurt her baby. She kept telling me not to drink. I'm not. I drink only fruit juice—party or not. I'm glad I didn't drink alcohol during my first pregnancy either.

No Tobacco

Cigarette smoke has many harmful substances including tars, nicotine, carbon monoxide, and lead. Smoking cigarettes causes babies to have lower-than-normal birth weights and to be born too early. The more you smoke, the greater your chances of having a baby with these problems. Also, try to keep away from smoky rooms because secondhand smoke is harmful, too.

If you smoke, stop smoking or cut down as much as you can as soon as you can. Ask your caregiver about finding a program to help you stop smoking. If you live with people who smoke, ask them to smoke outside so you don't have to breathe the smoke.

No Street Drugs

These drugs are not good for you—and they're definitely not good for your baby. You should avoid using any illegal or dangerous drug, especially during pregnancy.

Don't smoke marijuana. It affects your unborn baby as much as it does you. Carbon monoxide and nicotine in marijuana smoke decreases the amount of oxygen in your blood. So, your baby gets less, too.

Don't use cocaine or crack. They have an unhealthy effect on your brain and nervous system. They also affect your blood vessels. Reduced blood flow to important organs causes most of the bad effects of these drugs. They could make the placenta separate from the uterine wall or cause your baby to be born too early. Cocaine and crack can cause a stroke or heart attack in you or your baby.

Don't use meth. Methamphetamines (amphetamines) are uppers and may cause preterm labor and birth. They could also cause your baby to have a low birth weight, rapid heart rate, or very fussy behavior.

Don't take any illegal drugs. Drugs such as ecstasy, heroin, and other street drugs are just as bad or worse than the ones described before. If you're addicted to any drug, tell your caregiver. He or she can help you.

Watch Out for Harmful Chemicals and Toxins

These substances may cause birth defects, preterm labor, or *miscarriage* (death or delivery of a baby in early pregnancy):

- Pesticides (weed- and insect-killing sprays)
- Some cleaning agents or products
- Lead in water or paint
- Carbon monoxide
- Paint and paint thinners
- Mercury, benzene, and formaldehyde

Here are some ideas on how to avoid harmful chemicals around your home or workplace:

- Wash fruits and vegetables to help remove unsafe chemicals.
- If working with toxins, wear protective gear such as gloves or a mask. Or ask if you could be given other duties while pregnant.
- Let someone else do the painting, and stay away until the fumes are gone.
- Find out about the quality of your water by asking your local health department. Most water is safe. If your water isn't safe, drink bottled or filtered water during pregnancy.

Be Careful about Other Possible Hazards

Hot tubs and saunas. In early pregnancy, a high body temperature (over 100.4°F or 38°C) may cause birth defects in your baby. At other times in pregnancy, getting that hot may reduce blood flow to your uterus and baby. Therefore, avoid using hot tubs and saunas. You can take warm baths as long as you don't get too hot. If you begin to feel hot, get out of the tub.

Toxoplasmosis **(an infection caused by a parasite).** Cats spread the parasite through their poop. You can also get toxoplasmosis from eating raw meat or unwashed vegetables. If you've already had toxoplasmosis, your baby is safe because you can't get it again. If you get infected during pregnancy, you'll have cold-like symptoms. However, this infection will be more serious for your baby. It can cause deafness or other birth defects. Here's what can you do to avoid getting toxoplasmosis:

- Wash your hands after handling cats.
- Have someone else clean the litter box.
- Try not to work in a garden where cats may have pooped.
- Cook your meat well.
- Carefully wash all vegetables.

What Can You Do about Common Pregnancy Discomforts?

You'll probably have some of these normal (but irritating) discomforts during pregnancy. Try the following measures to help you cope with them. If you're worried, call your doctor or midwife for advice.

Nausea and Vomiting

It's common to feel sick to your stomach in the first months of pregnancy. This is sometimes called *morning sickness*, but it can happen anytime. You may feel like vomiting when you haven't eaten for several hours. Or your stomach may be upset when you smell strong odors such as smoke or food cooking. Sometimes, brushing your teeth may make you feel sick.

To help prevent nausea and vomiting, try these suggestions:

- Eat 5 or 6 small meals each day to avoid having an empty stomach.

- Whenever your stomach feels upset, eat something you think might help you feel better. It's usually whatever food or drink sounds good at the time.

- Wear wristbands (Sea-Bands) that apply pressure on an *acupressure point* (a sensitive area) on your wrist. Sea-Bands are usually used for seasickness, but they may help with morning sickness, too. Look for them at boating, travel, or sporting goods stores.

- Eat foods that contain ginger (for example, fresh ginger, ginger ale, ginger tea, or ginger cookies).

❦ Maria's Story ❦

In the first 3 months of pregnancy, I felt sick to my stomach almost every morning. My friend told me a great way to keep from vomiting. She told me to put some crackers by my bed so I could eat them as soon as I woke up. That really helped with the morning sickness. When I was queasy in the afternoon, I drank a glass of ginger ale. That made me feel better and it tasted pretty good. People at work joked about morning sickness. That made it a little easier to deal with. When you know almost every pregnant woman gets it, it's not so bad.

Heartburn

Heartburn (burping up stomach acid) is common in late pregnancy. It's caused by several factors. Pregnancy hormones relax the muscles at the top of your stomach and slow down the movement of food out of your stomach. Also, there's less room for food in your stomach as your baby grows. These suggestions may help you feel better:

- Avoid eating fatty foods and foods that produce gas or cause heartburn for you.

- Eat several small meals a day rather than a few large meals.

- Raise your head and shoulders with pillows, rather than lying flat in bed.

- Take antacids (acid reducers) or other drugs to control heartburn, but only if suggested by your caregiver.

Constipation and Hemorrhoids

Constipation (hard bowel movements) is common in pregnancy. By preventing constipation, you can relieve another common problem during pregnancy: *hemorrhoids* (swollen veins in your rectum). The following suggestions may help:

- Drink plenty of water and other fluids.
- Eat high-fiber foods such as fruits, vegetables, and whole-grain cereals and bread.
- Exercise (walk) each day.
- If these measures don't help, talk to your caregiver about taking high-fiber products to soften your bowel movements. Don't take laxatives.
- Some iron pills cause constipation. If you're taking iron pills, ask your caregiver if they could cause constipation and whether you could change to a brand that is less likely to cause hard BMs.

Backaches

You may get a backache as your growing belly changes your shape. Try to prevent back pain by following these simple suggestions:

- Try to have good posture to ease strain in your back. To improve your posture, stand as tall as possible, keep your chin level, and pull in your tummy.

- Be careful when lifting something heavy. Don't bend from the waist to pick it up. Bend your knees and hold it close to you as you stand up.
- Do exercises to strengthen your belly muscles and stretch your lower back muscles. (See the pelvic tilt exercise on page 57.)

You can help treat a backache by:

- Resting or sleeping more
- Getting a massage or back rub
- Using a cold pack or heating pad
- Taking a warm bath

How to Reduce Back Pain: The Pelvic Tilt Exercise

This exercise reduces lower back pain by strengthening the muscles in your belly.

1. Get on your hands and knees. Keep your back straight. (Do not sag.)

2. Tighten your belly muscles and raise your lower back toward the ceiling.
3. Hold for a slow count of 5 as you breathe out.

4. Relax your belly and let your back go flat again as you slowly breathe in.
5. Repeat 10 times.

Swollen Legs and Feet

To reduce swelling in your feet and legs, try these comfort measures:

- Walk or move around. Avoid sitting or standing for a long period. If you have to be on your feet for a long time, shift your weight from foot to foot or march in place.

- When you sit, try to move your feet every 10 minutes by stretching and flexing your ankles. Don't cross your legs at the knees.

- Rock in a rocking chair. This helps exercise the muscles in your legs and feet.

- When resting, put your feet up.

- Ask your caregiver about wearing support stockings. To prevent swelling, put them on in the morning before your feet are swollen.

- Drink plenty of water.

- Go swimming in a large pool or soak your feet in cool water.

Leg and Foot Cramps

Cramps (severe pain) in the muscles of your lower legs or feet are common in late pregnancy. They usually occur when you're resting or asleep. To prevent leg cramps, avoid pointing your toes or standing on your tiptoes. To prevent toe cramps, avoid curling your toes. Also, drink plenty of water during the day to help prevent muscle cramps at night.

To relieve a muscle cramp, slowly stretch the painful muscle by following these suggestions:

- To relieve a cramp in your calf, stand with your weight on the cramped leg. Keep your leg straight and your heel on the floor. Step forward with your other leg and bend that knee. Lean forward to stretch the calf muscle of the straight leg.

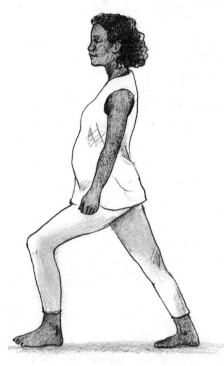

- To relieve a cramp in your foot, pull your toes up toward your shin (the front of your leg). This stretches your toes and the bottom of your foot.

Trouble Sleeping

It's common to not get a good night's sleep, especially in late pregnancy. If you can find time to exercise or take a walk during the day, it may help you sleep better at night. Don't exercise within 3 hours of bedtime.

At bedtime, try these suggestions to help you get to sleep:

- Take a warm bath.
- Drink a glass of warm milk.
- Have a massage.
- Listen to soothing music.

If you find yourself awake in the middle of the night, try using the relaxation techniques described on pages 44–45.

CHAPTER 4

Preparing for Birth

What should you do to get ready for labor and birth? This chapter suggests some things to do before your baby is born:

- Learn more about childbirth.
- Find out about your choices for your birth.
- Make a plan about what you want during labor.
- See the birthing rooms at your hospital or birth center.
- Get ready for the hospital or birth center by filling out forms and packing your bag.

What Choices Do You Have?

You'll be asked to make some choices about your care during childbirth. You may have fewer choices than you'd like to have, but you'll still have some choices. Many women take childbirth classes to learn about all the different types of choices. Most women also talk to their caregivers to find out possible options for their care. Learning about your choices helps you make realistic plans for your birth.

Choosing Your Childbirth Classes

Some hospitals, community groups, and prenatal clinics offer childbirth classes. These classes help prepare you for labor and birth. The best classes include the following things:

- Information about childbirth (what to expect and what you can do)
- Information about choices that are available to you and your *birth partner* (the person with you during labor and birth)
- A chance to practice ways of handling labor pain (for example, breathing techniques and comfort measures)
- Information about caring for your baby and yourself after birth
- Time to ask questions
- A chance to meet other people who are having babies

To learn where to go for classes, talk with your caregiver and friends. Since childbirth classes may fill up early, try to sign up before the 6th month of your pregnancy. There are fees for classes, but medical coupons in your state may pay for them.

One of the important benefits of taking classes is getting support from your fellow students. If you don't go to classes, talk with your caregiver or the clinic nurse to learn more about childbirth. Also, read this book to be better prepared for birth and early parenting.

Planning Your Birth

Getting ready for childbirth is like getting ready for any other big event in your life: You make plans. If you prepare for it, you'll know what to expect and will feel more in control. Begin preparing for birth by thinking about things that are important to you. Then make a list of your needs and wishes for your labor and birth. This is called a *birth plan*.

> ❧ *Maria's Story* ❧
>
> I was glad that John and I decided to take childbirth classes. He wasn't sure about being in the room with me during labor. But it was very important to me. In our class, we learned many things that John could do to help me during labor. The videos also helped us see what it would be like in the hospital. They made labor and birth seem less scary.

The Birth Plan

A birth plan is a letter to your caregivers (doctors, midwives, and nurses) describing your wishes, concerns, and how you'd like to be cared for during labor and birth. A birth plan tells your caregivers about you and your needs. It doesn't tell them what to do. Rather, it tells them about your wishes.

Here are some good reasons to write a birth plan:

- It encourages you to think about what you need and want.
- It helps you learn about your choices.
- It lets your caregivers know what's most important to you and why.
- It helps you work with your birth partners in planning the best birth experience possible.

It's a good idea to prepare your birth plan slowly over several weeks. It takes time to find out about your choices. Talk to other women about labor. Their birth stories may be upsetting, but they're usually helpful. In most childbirth classes, you'll hear about many birth experiences. Since every birth is different, it helps to be prepared for whatever may happen at your birth.

Your caregiver can tell you how the nurses will care for you during labor and birth. Also, talk to your caregiver about anything else you need to know (for example, how to get to the hospital if you don't have a car). Make a list of questions before your prenatal appointments. This will help you make the best birth plan for you.

When preparing a birth plan, you and your caregivers work together to make a general plan for a normal birth (labor and birth without medical problems). You also plan for any problems that may come up. This gives you a good idea of what to expect during childbirth and afterward. It also helps you learn important information about decisions you might have to make.

❧ Jenny's Story ❧

I wanted my mom to be with me at the hospital. She knew how much I hated needles. It helped when my sister gave me some ideas about what to ask for during labor. Luann loved the bathtub, and it made her labor go faster. I wrote about wanting to use the tub in my birth plan. I also said that I didn't want any needles if I could help it. Having a plan helped me feel prepared. I even had some ideas about what my boyfriend could do if he wanted to be there with me.

What Do You Put in Your Birth Plan?

Write down the choices that are important to you. It's helpful to think about the following questions when preparing your birth plan.

Information about You

- How old are you?
- Do you have other children?
- Are there customs of your native country, culture, or religion that may affect your labor and birth?
- Do you have special needs? A translator?
- Who will be with you during labor? Your partner? A friend? A family member? A doula? (See page 123 for information about doulas.)

Important Issues, Fears, or Concerns You May Have

- Are you concerned about modesty, vaginal exams, or other procedures?
- Are you afraid of needles or certain medical procedures?
- Are you worried about a past medical problem or birth experience?
- Are you concerned about anything for this birth experience?

Your Plans for Pain Relief and Comfort during Labor and Birth

- Do you want a *natural childbirth*? That is, do you want to avoid using drugs during labor?
- Do you want pain medicine? What kind? Narcotics and/or epidural? (See pages 132–135.)

- Do you want pain medicine as early as possible? Only if needed?
- How do you plan to cope with labor? Do you prefer relaxation and breathing techniques? Walking? Using a birth ball? Taking a tub bath? Other labor-coping skills? (See pages 109–128.)

Your Plans for Medical Care and Procedures during Normal Labor and Birth

- Do you have strong feelings about having (or not having) common medical procedures such as:
  * IV fluids throughout labor? (See page 93.)
  * Staying in bed with constant electronic fetal monitoring (EFM)? (See pages 91–92.)
  * Lying on your back for birth? Would you like to choose a birthing position? (See page 100.)
  * Episiotomy? (See page 151.)
- How would you like your caregiver and nurse to care for you during labor? Would you like the staff to stay in your room to comfort you? Would you like to be alone with your birth partner for part of your labor?

Your Plans for When Labor Doesn't Go as Expected

- Do you want labor to start by itself if possible? Do you want medical procedures such as induction? (See page 139.)
- What do you want to do if labor is long and slow? (See pages 147–152.)
- What are your plans if a cesarean birth is needed? (See pages 152–164.)
- What would you like to happen if your baby has a health problem or dies?

Your Plans for Caring for Yourself and Your Baby after Birth

- How will you feed your baby? Breastfeeding or formula feeding?

- Do you want your male baby circumcised?

- Do you have any concerns or thoughts about the normal newborn tests or procedures? (See pages 103 and 238.)

- Do you need certain foods or care because of customs of your family, religion, or native culture?

- Do you want the nurse to teach you about caring for your baby at home?

- Do you have any needs after going home? Help with buying food? Help getting medical care for you or your baby?

✹ Tanya's Story ✹

My first labor went *so* slow. This time I'd planned to walk around more. And I'd planned on not having an epidural. Everybody said, "If you take medicine too early, it makes labor longer." I had a doula this time, too. Jason did a pretty good job at Molly's birth. But it seemed like a good idea to have an extra person around who had more experience than Jason.

See page 72 for a blank birth plan. You can copy it and use it for your own birth plan.

Taking a Tour of Your Hospital or Birth Center

Most hospitals provide an opportunity to visit the birthing unit and see what it looks like. A good way to find out about a hospital's rules and procedures (called *routines*) is to ask about them while on a hospital tour.

Most birth centers want you to come in and see their rooms and furnishings. It's helpful to learn about the services that are available to you and your partner. To schedule a tour of your birth center, talk to your caregiver. He or she might go with you to the birth center or help you set up an appointment.

To schedule a hospital tour, call the education department or the birthing unit. A volunteer or educator often leads a scheduled tour. Tours typically involve seeing an empty birthing room and a postpartum room if it's separate from the labor-and-birth room. You can also see the nursery and the family waiting area. You usually don't see the room where cesarean operations are done.

The tour guide discusses some typical hospital routines and gives you a chance to ask questions. If your guide can't answer a question, you could ask to talk to one of the nurses. This information will give you an idea of what to expect at the hospital. Then you'll know more about your choices. Also, you'll learn if you can get the care you want.

Registering at the Hospital or Birth Center

Most hospitals and birth centers have you fill out admission forms before you come in to have your baby. Plan to read these forms before you're in labor so you have time to think about them. Then talk to your caregiver or the staff at the hospital or birth center. Ask questions about anything you don't understand. Discuss anything that makes you feel uncomfortable. Also, you may want to talk to a friend or family member about your questions and concerns.

You'll be asked to sign several forms. The general consent form allows the staff to care for you during labor (and care for you and your baby after the birth). You'll be asked to sign another form in the hospital if you or your baby needs a major medical procedure such as cesarean birth. In some hospitals, you may be asked to sign other consent forms for specific procedures such as epidural anesthesia. These forms allow you to make more choices about your care.

Your caregiver and the staff need to obtain your permission before taking care of you. This is called *informed consent*. It means that you were told about all your choices and the risks and benefits of each choice. You may be asked to make a decision or choice about a test, procedure, or type of medical care. So, ask as many questions as you need to help you and your partner feel comfortable with your decisions.

Packing Your Bag for the Hospital or Birth Center

Even though you'll be in the hospital or birth center for only a day or two (or less), you'll be happier if you have some of these personal items:

- This book
- Lip-gloss or balm
- Toothbrushes (for you and your partner) and toothpaste
- Personal comfort items (pillow from home, pictures, warm or cold packs, and so on)
- Warm socks in case your feet get cold during labor
- Nightgown (if you don't want to wear a hospital gown during labor)
- Pajamas or a nightgown that opens easily for breastfeeding
- Snacks for your partner
- Camera and film
- Phone numbers of people to call after the birth
- Tape or CD of relaxing music (Ask about available equipment.)
- Robe and slippers (Or use ones from the hospital.)
- Hairbrush, makeup, shampoo, or other toiletries
- Nursing bra
- Loose-fitting clothes (probably your maternity clothes) to wear when going home

- Clothes for the baby including an undershirt or "onesie" (one-piece body suit), diapers (cloth ones with waterproof cover, or disposable diapers), one-piece footed outfit, large lightweight blankets, warm (outside) blanket, and hat
- Car seat for safe ride home (properly installed in the car before you have your baby)

If you'll be giving birth at a birth center, you'll need most of these same items even though your stay will be shorter. If you're planning a home birth, ask your midwife or doctor about supplies and special preparations that you'll need in your home.

Birth Plan

Name _____ Due date _____

Doctor's or midwife's name_____

Birth setting (name of hospital or birth center)

_____

This is my plan for labor and birth. I want to let you know what is important to me. I know that this plan may have to change if problems come up. Thank you for your help and support.

Introducing myself:

Some helpful information about me:_____

_____

_____

Some information about my birth partner(s): _____

_____

_____

Important issues, fears, and concerns of mine: _____

_____

_____

My wishes for pain relief and comfort during labor and birth:

_____

_____

My wishes for medical care and procedures with normal labor and birth:

_____

_____

_____

_____

_____

My wishes if labor doesn't go as expected:

With a long, slow labor: _____

_____

_____

If my baby needs a cesarean birth: _____

_____

_____

If my baby has health problems: _____

_____

_____

My wishes for caring for my baby and myself after the birth:

Feeding my baby: Breast milk _____ Formula _____

My thoughts about baby care in the hospital/birth
center: _____

_____

_____

_____

Requests for special care or foods: _____

_____

_____

I want to learn about these things while in the
hospital/birth center: _____

_____

_____

_____

We need help with these things after we go home: _____

_____

_____

CHAPTER 5

Having Your Baby: Labor and Birth

Labor is the work done by your uterus when your baby is born. During labor, your uterus contracts and pushes your baby down onto your cervix. This opens the cervix. After the cervix is completely open, your pushing efforts and contractions move your baby down and out of the birth canal.

Childbirth (labor and birth) may take anywhere between a few hours and a few days. You can't know for sure how long it will take. It's different for every woman. Also, it's usually different for each woman each time she gives birth.

By the end of pregnancy, your uterus is the largest and strongest muscle in your body. When it contracts, your uterus hardens and bulges like any other muscle. If you press your fingertips on your belly during a contraction, you can feel how hard it is.

Contractions come and go during labor. Each contraction is like a wave: It's weak in the beginning; it builds to a peak; and then it gradually goes away. Between contractions, your uterus rests. As labor goes on, these rests get shorter and the contractions get longer and stronger.

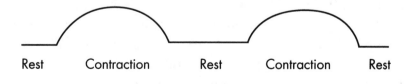

Rest   Contraction   Rest   Contraction   Rest

How Labor Begins

Hormones made by the mother and baby start labor. They set off a chain of events that cause:

- More uterine contractions
- Changes in the cervix (It becomes softer and thinner and begins to open.)
- Changes in the baby in preparation for life outside the womb

These hormonal changes usually work together at the time the baby is ready to be born and the mother is ready to give birth.

Luckily, most healthy women give birth to healthy *full-term* babies (babies born near their due dates). But what the mother does during pregnancy can affect when labor starts. For example, heavy smoking, having an infection, using street drugs, living with a lot of stress, or other factors can cause labor to start too early.

Medical Words Used When Talking about Labor

It's easier to understand what your caregivers are saying if you know some of the words they're using when talking about labor. Also, learning these words will help you as you read this book.

Changes in the Cervix

In late pregnancy, your cervix begins to change. These changes slowly prepare your cervix for labor. You and your caregiver can't see your cervix, but your caregiver can feel it during a vaginal exam. Changes in your cervix tell your caregiver how close you are to starting labor. During labor, your caregiver can check your cervix to find out how your labor is progressing.

This is how your cervix changes before and during labor:

- The cervix *ripens* (softens). During pregnancy, your cervix is firm. At the end of pregnancy, hormonal changes cause it to soften. Once your cervix is soft, it's ready to open. Cervical ripening may begin in the last weeks of pregnancy, or it could start just a few days before labor begins.

- The cervix *effaces* (thins or shortens). During pregnancy, the length of the cervix is about 1½ inches (3–4 centimeters). One centimeter is about this long:_____. In late pregnancy, the cervix becomes shorter and finally becomes almost paper thin. This process is called *effacement*. Effacement is usually measured in percentages: 0% effaced means that the cervix has not thinned at all (is still 4 centimeters long); 100% effaced means that it has thinned completely (is almost 0 centimeters long).

effacement:

| 0% | 50% | 90% | 100% |

dilation:

| 0 cm | 2–3 cm | 5 cm | 10 cm |

- The cervix *dilates* (opens). Although the cervix often begins to dilate before labor begins, most dilation takes place during labor. Dilation is measured in centimeters. When the cervix is opened only the width of a fingertip, it's 1 centimeter dilated. At the halfway point, it's 5 centimeters dilated. When the cervix is fully open, it's about 10 centimeters dilated.

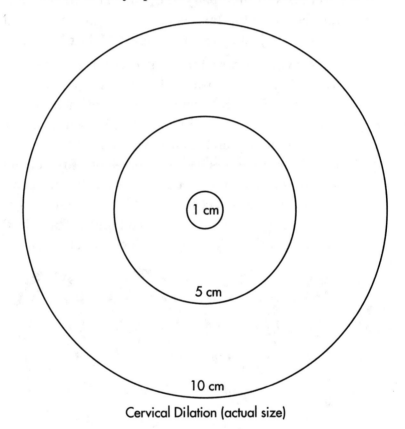

Cervical Dilation (actual size)

Timing Labor Contractions

Knowing how to time your contractions can help you decide if you're truly in labor. Then it's easier to know when to call your caregiver or when to go to the hospital or birth center.

Early Labor Record (sample)

Contractions on __April 29__

Time	Duration	Interval or Frequency	Comments
Starting time	How many seconds long?	How many minutes since the beginning of the last one?	Intensity of contractions, food eaten, breathing level, bloody show, status of membranes, other events
1:54 A.M.	40 seconds	–	Bloody show started at 6 P.M.
2:03 A.M.	45 seconds	9 minutes	Can't sleep
2:10 A.M.	45 seconds	7 minutes	Loose BM, backache
2:17 A.M.	50 seconds	7 minutes	Stronger!

You need to know 3 main terms to describe your contractions:

1. *Length* (how long a contraction lasts, in seconds)

2. *Frequency* (how often the contractions are coming—for example, every 5 minutes)

3. *Intensity* (how strong the contractions feel)

To time contractions, you need a watch or clock that tells the seconds. You also need a piece of paper or a blank early labor record such as the one above.

1. When a contraction begins, write down the time (include the hour, minutes, and seconds).

2. When the contraction ends, write down the time. Figure out the number of seconds that passed from the beginning of the contraction until the end of it. This tells you the *length* of the contraction.

3. To find out the *frequency*, time 5 or 6 contractions in a row. Figure out the number of minutes from the beginning of 1 contraction to the beginning of

the next. Do this for several contractions to find out how often they're coming.

4. To find out the strength or *intensity* of the contractions, compare the ones you're having now with the ones you had an hour ago. Do they seem stronger now? Are they more painful? If so, they're more intense.

Possible Positions for Your Unborn Baby

Head down facing your back

Head down facing forward

During most of your pregnancy, your baby moves around in your uterus. Your baby may even flip over. In the last month, your baby will kick and wiggle a lot, but she'll probably stay in the head-down position.

Most often, a baby gets into a head-down position with her face toward the mother's front or back. This means that her head will come out first when she's born.

It's possible for a baby's bottom or feet to come out first, but this is rare. This is called a *breech presentation*. Most doctors today do a cesarean operation to deliver breech babies because there are more problems when they come through the vagina. (See pages 152–164 for more on cesarean birth.)

Breech

During birth, your baby has to turn as she moves down the birth canal. This allows her head to fit through your pelvis. The turning movement is called *rotation* and the downward movement is called *descent*.

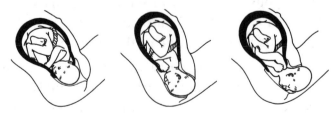

Rotation and descent

Stages of Labor

When talking about childbirth with your caregiver, you may hear these terms to describe the different stages of labor:

- *Prelabor*. These contractions occur before labor really begins. They help make the cervix softer and thinner. Because prelabor contractions don't usually open the cervix, this is sometimes called "false labor."

- *First stage*. These contractions work to open the cervix until it's dilated to 10 centimeters (completely open). This is sometimes called "true labor."

- *Second stage*. These contractions press your baby out of your uterus into your vagina. At this time, you push until your baby is born.

- *Third stage*. These contractions work to push out the placenta.

- *Fourth stage*. This refers to the first few hours after birth. It's also called *recovery*.

❧ Tanya's Story ❧

My friends told me a lot about their birth experiences. I noticed that each story was a little different. Some women hated labor. Others felt powerful and strong during labor. At my daughter Molly's birth, I was more afraid than I am with this baby. Last time, labor seemed scary, and that made the pain worse. I think I should've taken a birth class before Molly was born. I would have known more about what was happening.

> ❧ *Maria's Story* ❧
>
> I knew I was in labor when I couldn't talk through a
> contraction. It really hurt. When a contraction started,
> I had to stop everything except my special breathing.
> I needed that. The good thing about labor is that every
> contraction goes away, so you get a little break before
> the next one.

What Do Labor Contractions Feel Like?

Early in labor, contractions may feel like a dull lower
backache or menstrual cramps. They come and then
go away. These early contractions are usually (though
not always) short and mild. They come about every
15–20 minutes. However, some labors begin with strong
contractions that are closer together.

As labor advances, you'll feel the contractions in your
belly or in your lower back, or both. Many women feel
the pain begin in the back and come around to the front.
If your contractions keep coming but last less than 30
seconds, if they're not very strong, and if they don't
get closer together, you're still in prelabor or entering
early labor. In true labor, your contractions will become
stronger, longer, and/or closer together as time goes on.

How Do You Know When You're Really in Labor?

The following signs (or *physical symptoms*) will help you figure out if you're in labor. Some mean that you're in prelabor. Others tell you that your cervix is actually dilating and you're in labor.

✖ Jenny's Story ✖

In the beginning, labor contractions felt like big muscle cramps in my belly. And they kept coming every 10 minutes or so. You know how your arm muscles start to ache when you're holding something heavy for a long time? That's what early labor felt like for me. At the time, I thought it might feel like that until the baby was born. I was wrong.

Possible Signs of Labor

These signs may occur in prelabor or during the days before labor begins. Or you may not notice them until you're already having labor contractions. Since they're *possible* signs, you may have some or all of them:

- Vaginal mucus mixed with a little blood (called *bloody show*)
- Lower backache that may come and go
- Cramps (like menstrual cramps) in your lower belly
- Several soft bowel movements or diarrhea-like BMs
- Sudden burst of energy focused on getting ready for the baby (called the *nesting urge*)

Positive Signs of Labor

These are the clearest signs that labor has started:

- Contractions that get longer, stronger, and closer together as time goes on (These *progressing contractions* are painful and don't go away when you change your activity—for example, from walking to sitting down.)

- Leaking or a gush of water from your vagina caused by the bag of waters breaking

---

❧ *Cami's Story* ❧

When I was pregnant, all my friends who had babies wanted to tell me what labor felt like. One said, "You just gradually get into it. At first, it's hard to tell if it's labor or not. I thought I was in labor 3 or 4 times, but the contractions would just go away. Then, the day my son was born, they didn't quit. They just kept coming and coming, and then I knew. My belly got as hard as my head, and it hurt!"

Another friend said, "My bag of waters broke all at once—in our bed! I felt like I was peeing in my pants and couldn't stop. Then the contractions came hard and fast. No prelabor for me."

A third friend said, "I went to the hospital 2 times thinking I was in labor, but I wasn't. They kept telling me my contractions weren't close enough together to call it labor. When the contractions finally got to 5 minutes apart, I got to stay at the hospital."

When to Call Your Caregiver

During the last month of your pregnancy, ask your caregiver when you should call. Also, ask about where you should call. You may be told to call the hospital birthing unit (especially at night). Or you may be told to call your midwife or doctor directly. Here are some general guidelines:

- Call when your bag of waters breaks.

- Call when the contractions are intense (lasting a full minute and coming about every 5 minutes). You may want to call earlier if you've had a baby before.

- If your caregiver told you to call early because of a medical problem (or if you live far away), call as soon as you think labor has started.

- Call if you're anxious or have questions, even if you're not sure you're in labor.

Make sure you have someone who can drive you to the hospital day or night. Keep phone numbers handy. If you don't know anyone, choose a cab company and write down the number ahead of time. Keep enough cash in your purse or have your taxi voucher ready.

Getting through the First Stage of Labor

At some point, you'll go into labor (usually between 2 weeks before and 2 weeks after your due date). When labor starts, you're in the first stage of labor. This section describes how you might feel and what you'll be doing during the 3 different *phases* (or parts) of this stage. These phases are:

1. *Early labor.* This is the longest phase, but contractions are usually short and not very painful.

2. *Active labor.* Contractions are more intense.

3. *Transition.* This is the shortest phase, but contractions are most intense.

Your feelings will change as you go from one phase to another. Also, your coping skills will need to change as you move through each phase.

Early Labor

In the early phase of labor, contractions usually:

- Come every 6–20 minutes (They get closer together as time goes on until they're about 6 minutes apart.)

- Last 20–60 seconds (They become longer as time goes on until they last about 60 seconds.)

- Feel like strong menstrual cramps or mild pain in your belly and/or lower back

- Cause bloody show to pass from your vagina

During early labor, your cervix thins out and opens to about 4 centimeters. Your caregiver will do a vaginal exam and let you know how much you've dilated.

You'll probably spend most of early labor at home doing normal activities. You'll rest if it's nighttime and keep busy if it's daytime. Try not to do too much since you'll need plenty of energy for labor. You might also spend time wondering if you're really in labor. Keeping an early labor record like the one on page 79 will help you decide.

You'll probably feel excited and a bit nervous. Most likely, you'll want a family member or a friend with you.

What to Do in Early Labor

- Pack your bag (or prepare your home if you're planning a home birth).

- Go for a walk, listen to music, or watch a movie.

- If you're tired, try to rest.

- Use comfort measures to relax your muscles and calm your mind during painful contractions. (See pages 120–128 for more on comfort measures.)

- Have someone give you a back rub.

- Take a long shower (but *not* a long bath as it could slow labor progress at this time).

- Eat foods and drink beverages that are easy to digest, such as soup, fruit, yogurt, pasta, toast, juice, and herbal tea. Fatty foods aren't good at this time. They may upset your stomach.

When the contractions become painful and you can't walk or talk during a contraction, it's time to use your coping skills. (See pages 116–128 about how to do slow breathing and other comfort measures.) Try to stay relaxed, even limp, during the intense contractions. Keep your mind on calming thoughts, music, or pictures.

Between contractions, go back to whatever you were doing before the contraction. Try to be ready to focus on relaxing during the next contraction. In early labor, start working with your partner so he or she knows how to help you during the rest of your labor. Some women have an experienced woman (*birth doula*) come to their home to help them with early contractions.

✇ Jenny's Story ✇

I was at work when my contractions began. They got someone to replace me and someone else to take me to the hospital. But the nurse told me it was too soon to be in the hospital. So I had to wait for my mother to come get me. At home, I timed my contractions and packed my bag. The contractions stayed about the same for about 24 hours. When my contractions got stronger and were coming every 5 minutes, I knew it was time to go back to the hospital again. And I was right! I was 3 centimeters dilated.

Active Labor

Most women go to the hospital or birth center when they enter the active phase of labor. In active labor, contractions continue to become longer, stronger, and closer together. Contractions usually:

- Come every 4–5 minutes or less
- Last 60 seconds or longer
- Feel intense and painful

During this phase, labor speeds up and your cervix usually dilates faster than before. By the end of the active phase, your cervix is about 7–8 centimeters dilated.

In active labor, you become serious, quiet, and focused on your contractions. Earlier, your partner's jokes and talk were fun; now you can't listen. You don't want people asking you questions or talking to you during contractions. You may feel tired at this time. Most women feel like they can't keep going.

What to Do in Active Labor

- Move around. Try changing positions to get more comfortable (walking, standing, leaning on your partner or the bed, sitting, or lying in bed).
- Move, rock, or sway in rhythm (like slow dancing).
- Breathe in a rhythm during contractions.
- Relax between contractions.
- Go to the bathroom and empty your bladder about once an hour.

- Use whatever comfort measures you want.
  * Sit on or lean over a birth ball. (See page 127.)
  * Get into a tub or take a shower.
  * Drink water or suck on ice chips.
  * Listen to music.
- Remember that the pain of contractions is normal. It's not harmful.

Your partner should move in closer now. He or she should remain calm and share your serious mood. Your partner can help you stay with your breathing patterns and find comfortable positions. Your partner can also try softly touching or stroking you during this demanding phase of labor. What you need now is someone to help you feel safe, secure, and loved.

❧ Jenny's Story ❧

I didn't think I could do it. It was so hard. I cried. I told my mom, "I hate this! Get me drugs!" My mom never said yes or no. So, I just kept doing the same things. Every contraction, I stared at a picture of my cat and did the breathing. I moaned a lot, too. My mom kept telling me, "You're doing so well—just keep that rhythm." I hated labor, but after a while I knew I could do it. I stopped asking for drugs and kept my mind on the rhythm and my mom's voice.

Keeping You and Your Baby Healthy (Care in the Hospital)

When you give birth in a hospital, the nurses, doctors, and midwives use tests and procedures to check your progress and keep you and your baby safe. These common medical procedures are called *routines* because they're given to almost every woman who gives birth at that hospital. This section describes the most common tests and procedures for women giving birth in a hospital.

Checking on the Baby

This is also called *fetal monitoring*. One way to check on the baby's health during labor is to count the heartbeats of the baby (*fetus*) when the mother is having a contraction and right after the contraction is over.

There are 3 ways to do this:

1. The nurse listens to the fetal heartbeats by holding a *Doppler* (an ultrasound stethoscope like the one used during your prenatal visits) on your belly for about a minute. The heart rate is usually counted every 15–30 minutes during labor (and more often during the second stage).

2. With *external electronic fetal monitoring* (*EFM*), the nurse places 2 pieces of equipment on your belly and holds them in place with elastic belts. One piece keeps track of contractions. The other measures the baby's heart rate. Both pieces are connected to a machine that shows the information on a screen and makes a printed record.

3. *Internal EFM* may be used if the other methods have shown that your baby might be having a problem. Internal monitoring gives more information, but it's used only if needed. With internal EFM, 2 pieces of equipment are inserted through your vagina into your uterus. One is attached to the baby's head to measure the baby's heart rate.

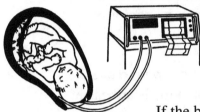 The other measures how strong the contractions are. As with external EFM, the 2 devices are attached to a machine that shows the information.

If the baby isn't getting enough oxygen from the mother's placenta, the heart rate changes. The medical staff uses this information to decide if they should do other tests or if treatment is needed.

A Reminder

Sometimes the stress of being in the hospital makes it hard to understand what your caregivers are telling you about your care. Remember that you can always ask for more information about any procedure before agreeing to have it done. If you still don't know why it's being done, ask again. It's your right to know what's happening to you.

Checking on the Mother

Throughout labor, the nurse checks many signs that tell about your health and how fast your labor is going. All test results are recorded in your hospital chart.

If you're having any problems, the following tests are done more often:

- The nurse watches and records your blood pressure, temperature, pulse (heart rate), urine output (how much you're peeing), and fluid intake (how much you're drinking or the amount of IV fluids).

- Vaginal exams help your nurse or caregiver check your labor progress (the thinning and opening of your cervix). Vaginal exams also help your caregiver know if your baby is moving down the birth canal.

- Your nurse or midwife will check the frequency and intensity of your contractions by either feeling your belly or using EFM.

Intravenous (IV) Fluids

IV fluid is water mixed with minerals given to you through a tube inserted in a *vein* (blood vessel below your skin) in your arm or hand. The fluid drips through the tube from an IV bag or bottle that hangs from a stand near the bed. An IV makes sure your body has enough fluids when you're not allowed to drink liquids. An IV is also a good way to give you medicine quickly if you need it. If you are in good health, you may not need an IV. You may want to drink water or juice instead.

Transition

This phase is usually the most difficult part of labor, but it's the shortest. For a first-time mother, transition is usually about 1 hour long. For mothers having another baby, it may be even shorter. These contractions aren't much more painful than those in the active phase, but they seem harder because they're longer and closer together. Contractions usually:

- Come every 2–3 minutes
- Last 1–2 minutes (Sometimes before one goes away, another one starts.)
- Feel very strong because the time is so short between them (30 seconds to 2 minutes)
- Come with new physical signs and strong emotions

These new physical signs help you know that you're in transition. You also know that labor is almost over and that your baby will soon be born. You may have some or all of these normal signs of transition:

- Bag of waters breaking (if it hasn't already) and more bloody show
- Pressure in your vagina and rectum that makes you want to grunt or strain hard, as if you're

having a bowel movement (However, it may be too early for you to push.)

- Nausea, vomiting, or hiccups
- Sensitive skin
- Feeling tired and sleepy between contractions
- Shaking of your legs or your whole body
- Changing back and forth between feeling cold and feeling hot and sweaty

Strong emotions often come with the intense physical signs of transition. You may feel:

- Overwhelmed, like you can't continue coping with the contractions
- Angry and afraid
- Grouchy and easily upset
- Ready to quit

Luckily, labor is almost over. You need to know that these feelings are normal. You also need to know that you and your baby are all right. This difficult time is usually short.

✖ Jenny's Story ✖

I told the nurse I was feeling pressure in my bottom. Then I got sick and threw up. Luckily, my mom had a little plastic dish to throw up in. I got the shakes, too. It was really hard. I panicked. The nurse told me to keep my eyes open and look at my mom. The nurse kept saying, "You're okay. This is the hardest part. Keep up with the rhythm." The nurse showed my mom how to give me a beat to follow with my breathing and moaning. It was all I could do just to follow my mom. It felt like it would never end, but it did. The next thing I knew I was making grunting sounds. I was glad when they told me it was time to push my baby out.

To get through transition without pain medications, use the same methods you used in the active phase. (See pages 89–90.) There's no need to remain calm and relaxed during these contractions. It may be easier if you make noise. However, it helps to stick with the same rhythmic movements and breathing pattern. This is called a *ritual* (doing the same things over and over to cope with the contractions). Between contractions, try to relax and rest, if only for a few seconds.

Your birth partner may be upset by your pain or the sounds you make and may not know how to help you. Your partner may think your coping sounds mean that you're suffering. Support and advice from your nurse and caregiver can help you both.

Your birth partner can help you by:

- Staying close to you (Some women like being held close. Others don't want to be touched at all, but want their partners to be within arm's reach.)

- Keeping your breathing rhythmical (counting your breaths or having you watch his hand as he gives you a steady beat)

- Helping you relax between contractions

- Giving you things to help you feel more comfortable (for example, a warm towel on your lower back or belly, a cool washcloth on your forehead, ice chips for thirst, pillows for support)

- Calling the nurse if you begin to grunt or hold your breath

During this phase, your cervix will dilate to 10 centimeters. This means your baby will now be able to slide through the cervix into your vagina. At the end of transition, it will be time for you to bear down and push your baby out.

✴ Tanya's Story ✺

My labor was different the second time. It was a lot
faster. Also, last time I had pain medicine and couldn't
feel anything. This time I felt pain, but I liked being
able to feel the pushing. When I got out of the tub,
I wished I hadn't because the contractions hurt more.
Then my water broke and went all over the floor.
I wanted to push right away, but the nurse told me
my cervix hadn't opened all the way yet. I wasn't
supposed to push, but I couldn't help it. I couldn't stop
even when I tried. The nurse got me onto my hands
and knees, which took away some of the pain and
pressure. But I still had to pant a little bit so I wouldn't
hold my breath and push. It was really hard. When
she told me to go ahead and push, it was such a relief!

Birth of the Baby: Second Stage of Labor

The second stage of labor begins after your cervix has dilated completely. In this stage, your baby moves out of the uterus, down the vagina, and is born. The second stage can be as short as 30 minutes, or it can take more than 3 hours.

In the second stage, you're more like your usual self than you were during transition. You have more energy. You're calmer and more relaxed. The contractions usually:

- Come every 3–4 minutes
- Last about 60 seconds
- Are less painful than contractions in transition
- Make you feel like pushing (The urge to push becomes stronger as your baby moves down the birth canal.)

What Is an Urge to Push?

The *urge to push* feels like a strong desire to grunt and bear down. You can't control it, just as you can't control a sneeze. Some women have an urge to push before full dilation. Others don't feel it until the cervix is 10 centimeters. Sometimes a woman never feels an urge to push. If you have epidural anesthesia, you'll feel numb and you probably won't feel a clear urge. (See pages 133–135 for more on epidural anesthesia.) With an epidural, you may feel some pressure or just feel different than before.

At the beginning of the second stage, you may not feel an urge to push. After 10–20 minutes, when the baby moves down into the vagina, the urge gets stronger. When you bear down along with the force of a contraction, it really helps move the baby down. Many women feel better when they push during contractions. Others think it hurts more. If it's painful for you, try another position. Also, it helps if you try to relax the muscles around your vaginal opening (*perineum*). Pushing works better and is less painful when your birth canal isn't tight.

The pressure of the baby in your vagina causes the urge to push. During each contraction, there are several urges. With each urge, you strain and bear down. Between the urges, you take a few breaths, then push again with the next urge. Between contractions, you won't have an urge to push. So, lean back and rest.

Maria's Story

I felt like I could push better if John helped me raise my shoulders and bend over my belly. I couldn't believe how hard my body made me push! It was hard work. My bottom burned, but it felt better if I pushed through the pain. John kept telling me to relax my legs. I knew that this was our secret way of reminding me to relax my bottom. It hurt less when I didn't tighten up.

Positions for Pushing

During pushing, use positions that feel most comfortable for you. Try several positions to find out which ones feel best. Your caregiver may ask you to try a new position to help the baby move down. Sometimes a different position is healthier for the baby. When it's time for the baby to be born, most caregivers want you to be sitting or leaning back.

Here are some possible pushing positions and why you may want to use them:

- Sitting and leaning back, as in a recliner, is a common birthing position called *semi-sitting*. It's easy for you to push in this position, and many caregivers like it best.

- Lying on your side may reduce back pain. It puts less pressure on your rectum or hemorrhoids.

- Squatting widens your pelvis and helps your baby move down the vagina. (Don't squat if you have an epidural, because you won't know if you're hurting your muscles and joints.)

- The hands-and-knees position decreases back pain. (Not needed if you have an epidural.)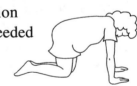

Your Baby Is Born

As your baby comes out, the head stretches open your vagina, and you feel it stinging or burning. Your caregiver may tell you not to push. To stop pushing, pant or blow out through your mouth. Remember to try relaxing your perineum and bottom.

The top of your baby's head comes out first, then her face. Once the head is born, it's a relief to have less pressure and pain. After the shoulders are out, the rest of the baby comes quickly. Your caregiver may suck fluids out of your baby's nose and mouth with a rubber suction bulb.

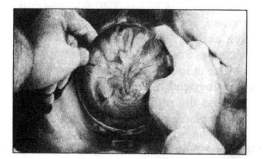

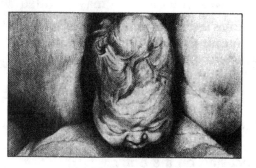

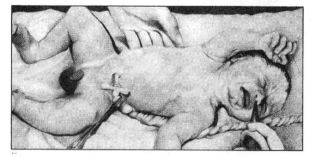

Delivery of the Placenta: Third Stage of Labor

After the birth, your baby is put on your belly and dried off. The umbilical cord is clamped and then cut. Your baby is wrapped in a warm blanket and put into your arms. As you get to know your baby, you wait for the placenta to come out.

This stage is the shortest and lasts about 10–30 minutes. The contractions aren't usually very painful. In fact, you may not notice them because you'll be busy looking at your baby. You may be asked to give a few pushes to get the placenta out. Then, if you've had an episiotomy or tear, your caregiver will stitch it closed. (For more about episiotomies, see page 151.)

The First Hours after Birth

Women have a variety of feelings after the birth. You may feel relieved that labor is over. You may feel proud of how well you did. You may be filled with love for your new baby, or surprised at how he looks. You may be amazed that you created such a wonderful baby. You may be full of energy, or you may feel tired and want to rest awhile.

Your partner may be overwhelmed with emotion and exhaustion at this time. Your partner and family members may hug you and cuddle your baby. You may all cry with joy.

Focusing on the Baby

Your baby may look bluish at first and may be streaked with blood. This is normal. A white, creamy substance (called *vernix*) may cover her body. This protected her skin while she was floating in the bag of waters. Your baby will begin breathing within seconds. Then her skin color will look more normal. Your baby's first cry will make everyone happy!

Right after birth, your nurse or caregiver will check your baby's well-being. This is called an *Apgar* test. If your baby's skin is pink and she's wiggling and crying, she's doing well. If your caregivers have any concerns, they'll massage her and possibly give her oxygen. If needed, they may take her to a nearby warming bed for more medical care.

If you plan to breastfeed your baby, try to begin in the first 30 minutes after birth. That is when your baby is alert and interested in feeding. Your nurse can help you. After feeding, your baby will be weighed and measured.

The nurse will check your baby's heartbeat, breathing, and temperature several times after birth. Sometime in the first hour, the nurse will put ointment in your baby's eyes to prevent an infection. Your baby will also get a vitamin K shot to prevent bleeding. If you have any concerns about the ointment or shot, talk to your caregiver before the birth. The nurse will give your baby a bath in the first couple of hours. This is usually done in the sink in your room.

In the first hour after birth, your baby is likely to be calm and alert with her eyes wide open. She'll notice new sounds, smells, and sights around her. If the light isn't too bright, she'll stare at your face. You can dim the lights or use your hand to make a shadow over her eyes to keep out the bright light. This is a good time to hold your baby and take a good look at her.

Recovery Time after the Birth

In the first hour or two after the birth, the nurse will check your blood pressure, pulse, and temperature often. After birth, you'll have a bloody vaginal flow like a heavy period. This is called *lochia*. You'll need to wear a maxi pad. To help reduce pain and swelling in your vagina, the nurse will place an ice pack on your perineum (under your pad). You can ask for pain medicine if you need it.

After birth, your uterus will continue to contract to close off the blood vessels where the placenta was. These contractions (called *afterpains*) are not usually very painful after the first baby, but they may be more painful after your second or third baby. Use slow breathing if you need help coping with the pain.

Breastfeeding causes more contractions and makes it seem like you're bleeding more. But you aren't bleeding more. The contractions are just pushing out the blood that was already inside your uterus. Actually, breastfeeding helps reduce the risk of bleeding too much and helps you heal faster. It takes several weeks for your uterus to return to its original size.

Your nurse or midwife will check your uterus to make sure it remains firm. If it's not, you may lose too much blood. If the top of your uterus is relaxed, the nurse will massage it to help make it contract. Because massage can be quite painful, you may want to check your uterus yourself. Ask your nurse to show you how to feel it. If it doesn't feel hard, you can massage it. This way you can keep your uterus firm with less discomfort.

Soon after the birth, your legs may shake. This is a common after childbirth. A warm blanket will help relieve the trembling. The shaking will go away in a short time. You may also feel hungry and thirsty. This isn't surprising since you've been working hard and probably missed some meals. Ask for something to eat and drink.

You'll probably feel relief that labor is over—and excitement that your baby is here. As your baby cuddles with you and looks into your face, you'll fall in love with her. These moments help you bond with your baby. Your partner will also want to hold and enjoy your baby.

CHAPTER 6

What about Pain during Labor?

This chapter tells you many things you can do for yourself to reduce labor pain. It also describes medicines for pain relief.

What Causes Pain during Labor?

When new mothers talk about how labor felt, they describe it as painful, exhausting, frightening, and amazing. Most pregnant women worry about the pain. Several things cause the pain of childbirth:

- Hard work by the muscles of your uterus during contractions
- Opening of your cervix
- Pressure on and stretching of your birth canal

The feeling of labor pain is different for each woman. Some women feel more pain than others during labor. Several things affect how much pain you feel:

- Your past experience with pain
- How healthy you are
- How long your labor lasts and how tired you feel
- Whether you have a birth partner or not
- Your ability to use coping skills to handle the pain
- Use of pain medicines

Fear makes your pain worse. If you know labor pain is normal, you'll probably feel less pain because you're not so afraid of it. Pain during labor does not mean that something is wrong (like the pain caused by an injury or illness). Pain is a normal part of the birth process. It usually means that the baby is closer to being born.

Knowing several pain-coping methods helps you feel less afraid. Using these skills during labor helps you feel more powerful.

Skills for Coping with Childbirth Pain

There are many ways to cope with the pain and stress of labor. These coping skills and comfort measures may be used for your entire labor. Or you can use them to ease your pain in early labor and then use pain medicines if or when they're needed.

Coping well during labor means that you're not overwhelmed or panicked by the contractions. It means that you're able to relax and handle the pain, even when you can't make it go away. The most helpful labor-coping skills include:

- Relaxation
- Rhythmic breathing and movement
- Comfort measures (and focusing your mind on them)

Use Relaxation to Reduce Pain

Women who cope well in labor use relaxation. They try to relax during the contractions and especially between them. Some women let their muscles go limp during contractions and then move around between contractions. Some women are more active during contractions (swaying or rocking) and relax and rest only between contractions. The point is that you should do whatever is relaxing for you at that time of labor.

Relaxation (letting go of muscle tension) is an important part of coping with labor. During labor, relaxation can help in several ways. It can:

- Save your energy (so you don't get so tired)
- Calm your mind
- Reduce your stress and fear
- Decrease your pain

Relaxation keeps you from tightening your muscles. When you relax, you decrease tension that makes the pain worse. Also, when you're trying to relax during a contraction, you're thinking about not tightening up instead of thinking about the pain.

The ability to relax comes more easily to some than to others. With practice, however, you can learn to relax. Start by doing the "Learning to Relax" exercise on page 45. Then practice the "Relaxing While You're Resting" exercise on page 111. Once you know how to relax, learn the skills you'll use during labor—the "Relaxation Countdown" (page 112) and "Relaxing Tension Spots" (page 114). Then practice them so you can easily do them during labor. You'll feel good knowing that you have the power to relax whenever you need to reduce your stress.

When you begin practicing relaxation, lie down on your side with plenty of pillows. Or sit in an easy chair with your head and arms supported. Make yourself comfortable. After you've learned to relax in these positions, practice relaxing while sitting up, standing, or walking. You'll need to relax in these positions during labor.

When you're learning relaxation skills, begin in a quiet, calm place. Try using 1 skill each night before falling asleep. Your goal is to have full body relaxation before you finish the exercise. When you can do this, then try it in noisier, more active settings. Remember that hospitals are busy places and labor can be stressful.

Relaxing While You're Resting

With this exercise, you relax your muscles while taking a rest. You can read this exercise to yourself and think about it as you practice. Or you can have your partner read it to you while you listen. First, you'll *focus* on (think about) an area and then try releasing tension there. Relax your muscles in each area as your attention moves from your feet up to your head.

1. Find a comfortable position lying on your side or sitting in a chair. Make sure your head, arms, and legs are supported.

2. Close your eyes and breathe slowly.

3. Think about your toes and feet. Just let go of tension there.

4. Now focus on your legs. They feel comfortable. Think of your legs as warm and relaxed.

5. Focus on your lower back. Imagine that someone with warm hands is giving you a back rub. Feel the warmth. Feel the tension leaving.

6. Pay attention to your chest. As you breathe in, your chest swells easily, making room for the air. As you breathe out, your chest relaxes to help the air flow out. Breathe slowly and let the air flow in and out. This easy breathing helps you relax more.

7. Focus on your arms. Let go of tension. Relax down your arms to your hands and fingers.

8. Now focus on your neck and shoulders. Your head feels heavy. Feel the tension slipping away.

9. Think about your face. Your jaw is relaxed. Your eyelids are heavy. You have a calm, peaceful expression on your face. This means you're also calm and peaceful on the inside. Take a few moments to enjoy this calm feeling.

10. Now it's time to end this relaxation session. Gradually open your eyes, wiggle your toes, stretch, and get up slowly.

Relaxation Countdown

During labor, you may want to use the relaxation countdown to relax between contractions. However, you can use it whenever you want to quickly release muscle tension during a busy day. It can also help you get back to sleep at night. The relaxation countdown is like a wave of relaxation from your head down to your toes. As you practice, use as many breaths as you need to relax your whole body.

1. Sit in a chair or lie down. Close your eyes.

2. Be aware of your breathing. Try to make your breathing slow and relaxed.

3. Breathe in through your nose and out through your mouth. With each out-breath, think *relax* and release any tension in your muscles.

4. Now focus on relaxing different areas of your body with each breath. Think about an area when you breathe in. Let go of any tension there when you breathe out:

   - Neck and shoulders
   - Arms and hands
   - Chest and belly
   - Back and hips
   - Legs and feet

5. Notice how you feel. Enjoy the relaxation and the release of tension.

Trying to relax during a labor contraction helps decrease your pain even if you aren't totally relaxed. It's easier to relax 1 area of your body than to relax your whole body. So, learn the "Relaxing Tension Spots" exercise on page 114 to help with relaxation during labor. When doing this technique, use slow breathing to help you relax. Focus on 1 tension spot with each breath. Or you can take 2 breaths if needed. Think of each out-breath as a relaxing breath.

When practicing and during labor, you may want your partner to help you relax your tension spots. If so, have your partner tell you what area to relax. Or have your partner touch a spot that's tense. Then focus on that area and release tension during your slow out-breath. This is called *touch relaxation*.

Relaxing Tension Spots

You may want to use this technique during labor contractions. Focus on areas that you tighten when you're under stress. For example, many people tense their shoulders or tighten the muscles in their neck. Some clench their jaw; others frown or have a worried look. These are their tension spots. Do you know your tension spots?

1. Sit or lie down. Get comfortable.

2. Breathe in slowly and easily through your nose. Look for tension in 1 area of your body.

3. Breathe out through your mouth. Release any tension from that spot.

4. With your next in-breath, focus on a nearby area of your body.

5. Check for tension on the in-breath, and release it on the out-breath.

6. Slowly move your attention from 1 area to another:
   - Face and jaw
   - Neck
   - Shoulders
   - Arms (one at a time)
   - Upper back
   - Lower back
   - Hips and buttocks
   - Legs (one at a time)

During a contraction, you probably won't be able to move through all these areas of your body. So, relax as many as you can during 1 contraction. Then go to the others during the next contraction.

Women who use coping skills such as relaxation and breathing usually feel less pain than women who don't use them. These skills can also be helpful at other times in your life. If you learn them now, you can teach your child to relax and breathe with the pain of a hurt knee or a sore finger. Or you can help yourself or your child through a painful medical procedure such as getting a shot.

Use Rhythmic Breathing and Movement to Reduce Pain

During labor contractions, try to breath in patterns that have a steady beat. Plan to use rhythm when you breathe, moan, or chant. During a contraction, try to combine your special breathing patterns with rhythmic movements. Also, plan to rock, sway, or even dance in rhythm during labor contractions.

Breathing Patterns for Labor

Breathing patterns are used in labor to help you relax. They also help you and your baby get plenty of oxygen. In addition, they help you focus on keeping a rhythmic beat for your breathing. By practicing a variety of breathing patterns before labor, it will be much easier to use them during labor.

If you don't feel like you need to do anything special to handle the pain of contractions, just breathe normally. When you feel like you need some help to cope with the pain, then begin using a special breathing pattern during each contraction. Many women begin using a breathing pattern when labor contractions are intense and definitely painful. They can't keep walking or talking. They have to stop what they're doing and just breathe until the contraction is over.

There are 2 basic patterns of breathing: slow breathing and light breathing. Once you learn these patterns, you can combine them to make new ones.

How to Use Breathing Patterns during Labor Contractions

1. When a contraction begins, take a big, relaxing breath.

2. You may want to keep your eyes open or closed. If open, look at a person or object.

3. Relax your muscles as much as you can. With every out-breath, try relaxing more.

4. Breathe in a rhythmic pattern through the contraction.

5. Focus on a comfort measure:

   - Look at something

   - Talk silently to yourself, such as counting your breaths

   - Move in rhythm

   - Release muscle tension

   - Enjoy the warmth of a shower or bath

6. At the end of the contraction, take a relaxing breath. Release all your tension as you breathe out.

Slow Breathing

Begin using slow breathing when it's hard to walk or talk during a contraction. Use this breathing pattern as long as you can. You may use it through your entire labor. Or you may need to switch to light breathing if contractions become too hard to get through with just slow breathing. During labor, plan to do whatever works for you.

Breathing→

Contraction→

How to Use Slow Breathing in Labor

1. Slowly breathe in through your nose. Then slowly breathe out through your mouth. (If your nose is stuffy, breathe in and out through your mouth.)

2. Breathe in quietly. Your out-breath should sound like a relaxing sigh (like a sigh of relief). In labor, you may moan or say words as you breathe out.

3. Keep your shoulders relaxed and comfortable.

4. Have your mouth slightly open and relaxed.

5. Breathe about 6–10 times per minute (about half your normal breathing rate).

The most important thing is that the slow breathing is comfortable and relaxing for you. Practice this pattern until you can do it easily. Try to do slow breathing for 60–90 seconds at a time, because in labor the contractions last about that long.

Light Breathing

In labor, light breathing is used when you have trouble relaxing or keeping a rhythm using slow breathing. You may find that you naturally speed up your breathing when contractions become more painful. If you keep tightening your hands into fists at the peak of every contraction, switch to light breathing. Let the intensity of your contractions guide you in deciding when to use light breathing.

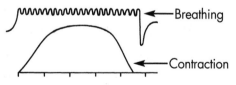

How to Use Light Breathing in Labor

1. Breathe in and out through your mouth.

2. Keep your breathing shallow, quick, and light. Think about using only the top part of your lungs.

3. When you breathe out, make a short blow with a light sound such as *hoo* or *hee*. Use the sound you like best.

4. Let your body take care of the in-breaths. They should be quiet. But you should hear the out-breaths.

5. Keep your mouth and shoulders relaxed.

6. Take a breath every 1 or 2 seconds. Pause for a short time after each out-breath so air can come back into your lungs.

7. Make each breath about the same. Keep the same beat or rhythm.

This pattern is not as easy to learn as slow breathing. At first, you may feel tense, as if you can't get enough air. Practice it for 1–2 minutes at a time until you feel you can do it without feeling short of breath. If you feel short of breath, slow your breathing down a bit. Make sure to relax your shoulders and wait a little longer before taking another breath. Some women say that light breathing is easier to do in labor. Your pain and the intensity of your contractions will guide your breathing rate during labor.

Light breathing may make your mouth dry. To keep from feeling thirsty, try these suggestions:

- Between every contraction, sip water or suck on ice chips or a frozen juice bar.

- After several contractions, brush your teeth, rinse your mouth, or use lip balm or ointment during a rest between contractions.

Other Breathing Patterns

Some women combine slow and light breathing to make new rhythmic patterns.

1. One way is to take 3 light breaths and then a long, slow one. It would look like this:

2. Another way is to start with slow breathing and change to light breathing at the peak of a contraction when it's most painful. It might look like this:

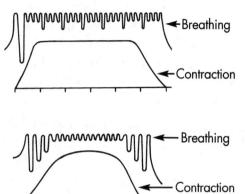

How to Practice Breathing Patterns

During the last months of your pregnancy, try to practice each breathing pattern 2–3 times a week.

- Use different positions such as sitting up, lying on your side, standing, being on your hands and knees, and even riding in a car.

- Then add relaxing comfort measures such as attention-focusing or movement. (See pages 124–128.)

By practicing, you'll be prepared to use breathing patterns during labor. You may or may not use all of them, but learning them gives you more options for coping with labor pain. Having choices can make you feel more powerful and in control of your labor.

❧ Jenny's Story ❧

When the pain got pretty bad, Mom was right in my face, nodding her head up and down and making me breathe with her. I didn't think I could keep going, but I guess I moved along really well. I didn't even have a chance to think about drugs for pain. When I got to push, all I wanted to do was get the baby out. And I did! I can't believe I did it without drugs. And I didn't regret it one bit. I'm proud of myself. My little girl was wide-awake, and she looked right at me when she heard my voice.

Use Comfort Measures to Help You Handle Pain

As you prepare for labor, learn the comfort measures in this book and use them when you need them. Also, think about things you do to make yourself feel better and try to do them during labor. How would you answer these questions?

- What helps you relax now? (Is it music, massage, a bath, a shower, or thinking about pleasant places and activities?)

- What helps you feel safe and comfortable? (Is it a soothing voice or your favorite pillow, CD, or photo?)

- What person or people do you want by your side during labor?

Having a Birth Partner

You'll feel more secure if you have a familiar person with you during labor. Also, contractions may seem less painful if that person is with you. During your pregnancy, choose the person you'd like as your birth partner. Some women have more than one. Your birth partner may be the baby's father, your mother, a relative, a friend, or a doula.

What Does a Birth Partner Do?

Your birth partner can help you before the birth by:

- Going to childbirth classes with you
- Listening to you when you talk about your needs and plans for your birth
- Helping you write a birth plan

Your birth partner can help you during labor by:

- Helping you pass the time during early labor (walking, playing cards, listening to music, talking, and so on)
- Staying with you throughout labor and birth
- Timing contractions
- Helping you relax during and between contractions
- Helping you cope as needed during contractions:
    * Keeping a rhythm for your breathing
    * Helping you use different positions and movement
    * Helping you focus your attention away from the pain

- Providing or suggesting comfort measures such as:
    * Giving you a back rub
    * Offering sips of water or ice chips
    * Helping you get into a tub or shower
- Staying calm and reassuring
- Offering encouragement when needed
- Helping you feel safe and loved
- Sharing in the joy of birth

If you're going to have more than 1 birth partner, decide what each person's role will be. The one who attended prenatal classes with you may be best at helping you with relaxation and breathing patterns. A family member may be best at offering love and support. A doula may be best at suggesting coping skills and calming both you and your partner. By writing down everyone's role in your birth plan, you'll avoid confusion and be more likely to enjoy your birth experience.

❧ Maria's Story ❧

John and I walked the halls in the hospital during my labor. Because I was having a lot of back pain, I also spent a lot of time on all fours swaying my hips. It really helped when John pressed on my back during a contraction. While John was pushing on my back, Cindy, my nurse, helped me with my breathing. It was really great to have them both helping me.

What Is a Doula?

A *doula* is a woman who's trained to help you and your partner by giving support and easing your pain and worries during childbirth. Doulas are experienced in "mothering the mother." Most professional doulas charge a fee for their services. Many of them have a sliding scale to allow all women to have a doula if they want one. Also, some hospitals have doulas on staff, and there's no charge to you.

The doula's role is to help you have the most satisfying birth possible. She stays with you from the time you call her until 1–2 hours after the birth. She helps you in the ways you want to be helped. She may be your only birth partner, or she may help your loved one or friend with ways to comfort you.

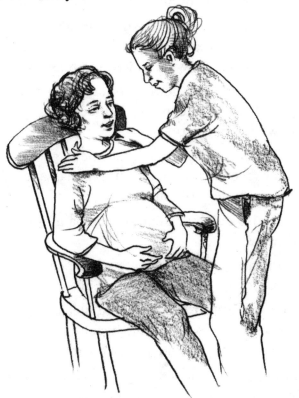

Focusing Your Attention

During labor contractions, you'll want to focus your attention on something. Some women find it helpful to "tune in to" the pain. They focus on it and change their activities to respond to it. Other women think of something other than the pain. For example, they focus on what they're doing or what their partner is doing. Or they think of something else to get their minds off the pain.

To help get your mind off the pain, try focusing on what you notice with your 5 senses:

- *Sight*. Look at something such as your partner's face, a picture, or a toy for the baby.

- *Sound*. Listen to your favorite music, a soothing voice, or the rhythmic pattern of your breathing.

- *Touch*. Pay attention as your partner touches or strokes you during a contraction. Touching a tense place may remind you to relax.

- *Taste*. Keep from getting thirsty by drinking sips of water or chewing on ice chips between contractions.

- *Smell*. Bring something that smells good to you (your favorite lotion, a soothing massage oil, or even a piece of lemon).

You can also get your mind off the pain by focusing on other things:

- Think about the words of a song, poem, or prayer. Or say or sing them out loud.

- Picture yourself in a calm and pleasant place (for example, lying on the beach, walking in the park, or sitting in a cozy chair).

- Count your breaths during each contraction (or have your partner do it). This helps you know when you're near the end of a contraction.

- Focus on relaxing an area of your body with each out-breath. (See "Relaxing Tension Spots" on page 114.)
- Move your body in rhythm. For example, rock in a chair, move back and forth on a birth ball, or stand and sway from side to side. (See page 127 for more information.)
- Be creative. Think of other things that would work for you.

As you practice the breathing patterns and relaxation skills before labor, try these attention-focusing methods. You'll probably like some of them more than others. Be ready to use them in labor. Also, during labor you may find something that helps even more than the things you practiced.

Using Massage and Touch

Having a massage can be soothing and relaxing during pregnancy and labor. Having your neck, shoulders, back, feet, and hands massaged can be very comforting. You may also enjoy a firm, stroking touch on your arms, legs, or back. Lightly stroking your belly may feel good during contractions, too.

Remind your partner to massage and stroke you in a relaxing rhythm. Work with your partner before labor to find out what kind of massage and touch is most helpful to you. Plan to use your favorite kinds in labor. You may prefer one or more of the following:

- Light, tickly touch
- Firm stroking
- Squeezing and letting go of muscles such as those in your shoulders or upper arms
- Firm massage or back rub

Using Baths and Showers

Being in warm water is very comforting for most women during active labor. Contractions are usually less painful if you're in water. A shower or whirlpool bath may help you relax by providing a gentle massage. Find out if you can take a bath or shower during labor in your hospital or birth center.

Using Warm and Cold Packs

A warm pack on your lower back or belly can be very soothing. A warm pack is simply a washcloth or small towel soaked in very warm water, wrung out, and quickly put wherever you need it. As it cools, replace it with another warm one. A warm blanket can also help if you feel chilly.

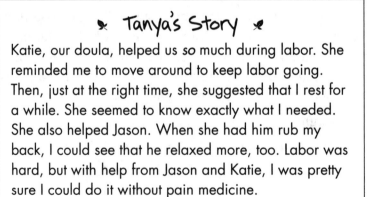

A cold pack helps reduce back pain during labor. Examples of cold packs include a rubber glove filled with crushed ice, a bag of frozen peas, or a frozen gel pack like the ones used for sports injuries. Wrap the cold pack with a thin towel to protect your skin.

> ### ❧ Tanya's Story ❧
>
> Katie, our doula, helped us *so* much during labor. She reminded me to move around to keep labor going. Then, just at the right time, she suggested that I rest for a while. She seemed to know exactly what I needed. She also helped Jason. When she had him rub my back, I could see that he relaxed more, too. Labor was hard, but with help from Jason and Katie, I was pretty sure I could do it without pain medicine.

Using Different Positions and Movement

Moving around during labor can help with pain. Also, changing your position every 30 minutes may help speed up a slow labor. Try these positions:

- Sitting

- Standing

- Lying down (on your side or leaning back in bed)

- On your hands and knees

Being upright for part of your labor gives you a greater sense of control than always lying down. However, try to use some restful positions, too. Try alternating between periods of resting and times when you're more active.

Rhythmic movements provide comfort, too. For example:

- Walking

- Swaying from side to side

- Rocking

- Using a big ball like the ones used in exercise classes (Some hospitals have these "birth balls." You can sit on one and sway during contractions. Or you can place it on the bed and lean over it for support.)

- Doing any other rhythmic movements that help you cope with labor pain

Drinking Enough Fluids

Most women are thirsty during labor. Between contractions in early labor, try to drink something (water, tea, or juice). In active labor, you may not want to drink as much. So, take small sips of water, chew on ice chips, or suck on a frozen juice bar.

If the nurses tell you not to drink anything, or if you're vomiting, they'll give you IV fluids. (For more on IV fluids, see page 93.) Even with IV fluids, you may have a dry mouth. Try sucking on ice chips or a sour lollipop, brushing your teeth, or rinsing with cold water or mouthwash.

Remember to go to the bathroom about once every hour. A full bladder may slow your labor progress. It also increases pain.

Ways to Cope with Back Pain during Labor

Some positions and movements can be very helpful if you have severe back pain during labor. Back pain is usually caused by the baby's head putting pressure on the back of your pelvis. If the back of the baby's head presses on your lower backbones during contractions, you have more pain. When the baby turns around (rotates), back pain usually goes away.

Positions to Help Reduce Back Pain

Positions that keep the baby away from your back usually decrease back pain. You should avoid lying on your back, if possible. When you lie on your back, the baby stays against your backbone and his head puts more pressure on it. Positions that make you feel better are:

- *Being on hands and knees*. Adding rocking movements while on hands and knees may help the baby move around to a position that causes less pain.

- *Leaning forward*. Try leaning forward while sitting, standing, or kneeling. You can lean over a birth ball, the labor bed, or against a chair.

- *Walking, swaying while standing, and stair climbing*. Movement helps the baby rotate. Being upright also helps the baby move down (descend) into your pelvis.

- *Side-lying*. Try lying on 1 side and then the other. Find out which side is more comfortable. Roll forward onto pillows. You might have less back pain.

Back Pressure by Your Partner to Reduce Back Pain

Your birth partner can also help reduce your back pain by pressing on your back. Pressure from the outside keeps your pelvis in the right position. This *external* (outside) pressure balances the *internal* (inside) pressure caused by the baby's head. To use back pressure during a contraction, your partner can:

1. Hold the front of one of your hip bones with one hand, to keep you from being pushed forward.

2. Press firmly with the heel of his or her hand in one spot on your lower back or buttocks.

3. Keep the pressure steady for the whole contraction.

4. Rest between contractions.

5. Ask you how the pressure feels.

6. Stop pressing if the pressure isn't helping or if it hurts you.

You'll probably know what spot needs the pressure. But the exact spot may change as the baby moves down into your pelvis. If you're not sure where your partner should push, have him or her press in different spots during each contraction. Tell your partner what feels best.

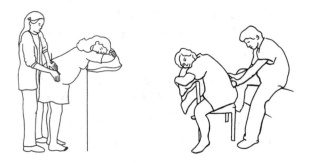

❧ Maria's Story ❧

I had a lot of back pain during labor. I used the birth ball quite a bit. I also moved back and forth. When contractions started to really hurt, John pushed on my back while Cindy, my nurse, held my hand. We did that for over an hour. Then Cindy checked my cervix again. I was dilated to 8 centimeters! I stayed on my side for a while and rested. Then it was back to the birth ball and rocking chair. When my baby finally moved around, I didn't like having my back pressed anymore. John was glad because his arms were sore.

Pain Medicines Used during Childbirth

How do you decide whether to take pain medicines? Some women know that they want to have a *natural childbirth* (giving birth without using medicine). They plan on using labor-coping skills when contractions become painful.

Some women aren't sure about using pain medicines. If they do use them, they don't want to take too many. They can cope with some pain, but they don't want to suffer. Other women know for sure that they want a pain shot or an epidural during labor.

It's a good idea to learn the coping skills described on pages 109–130 even if you plan to use medicines. These skills can help you at home while you're in early labor. They can also help you while you wait to get your pain medicine at the hospital. Most women who choose pain medicines are glad they had ways of helping themselves before getting the medicine or epidural.

Plan to talk to your caregiver about pain medicines during one of your visits in late pregnancy. The pain medicines used during childbirth relieve your pain, but they also affect your baby and your labor. Because of this, caregivers choose drugs that help you the most and have the fewest bad effects.

Medicines used for labor pain either take away some pain or take away all the pain. The most common types of pain medicines for labor and birth are *narcotics*, an *epidural*, and *local anesthesia*.

Narcotics

These medicines affect how your brain responds to pain signals from your body. They don't take away all the pain, but they reduce the pain you feel. You may not notice the pain at the beginning or end of a contraction, but you'll still feel it at the peak of a contraction.

How Are Narcotics Given?

Narcotics are given by *injection* (a shot into a muscle, an IV line, or directly into your vein). The medicine goes into your bloodstream and through your body. These drugs also go to your baby. When a narcotic is given as an epidural or spinal drug, the effects are different. (For more on epidurals, see pages 133–135.)

How Do Narcotics Help You?

- Narcotics are sometimes used in long prelabor to stop contractions and give you a rest.
- They may be given in active labor to decrease pain and promote relaxation.
- Narcotics are often used for pain relief after a cesarean birth. (See pages 161–162.)

What Are the Side Effects of Narcotics?

- They may make you sleepy, dizzy, or sick to your stomach.
- Narcotics can slow labor if given in early labor.
- Narcotics may affect your baby in the first hours after birth. Your baby may be sleepier than a baby whose mother did not take narcotics. Also, your baby may need more help with breastfeeding or have a slower breathing rate right after birth.
- Narcotics used after a cesarean birth may cause constipation.

Epidural

Epidural anesthesia numbs your body from your waist to your hips because the medicine is put near the nerves of your *spine* (backbone) in that area. Epidurals usually take away almost all of the pain. You may not even notice that you're having contractions. Or you might feel like you're having mild contractions similar to ones when labor began.

How Is an Epidural Given?

Drugs are given through a tube that's placed near your backbone in your lower back.

1. You lie on your side with your body curled, or you sit up leaning forward.

2. The doctor (an *anesthesiologist*) washes your lower back and numbs your skin with a shot of *local anesthetic*.

3. A needle is inserted near your backbone in the epidural space. A thin plastic tube is then inserted through the needle. The needle is removed, but the tube remains in place, taped to your back.

4. The tube is connected to a machine that slowly drips the medicines into the epidural space.

5. Within a few minutes, you begin to notice the effects (tingling, numbness). Within 15–20 minutes, the pain will probably be almost gone.

How Does an Epidural Help You?

- An epidural gives you good pain relief by numbing your belly and back. Very little medicine goes to your baby.

- It allows you to sleep if you're tired.

- Epidural anesthesia is sometimes given for a cesarean birth instead of spinal anesthesia. (*Spinal anesthesia* uses similar medicines, but it's given as a shot into the spinal fluid near your spinal cord.)

What Are the Side Effects of Epidurals?

- An epidural may slow labor progress if given too early.

- The numbing effect of an epidural may cause a drop in your blood pressure.

- Your body temperature may change, giving you a fever, especially if you've had an epidural longer than 6 hours.

- Usually you can't walk when you've had an epidural.

- You may have trouble changing positions. And it may be harder to push your baby out when you've had epidural anesthesia.

Because epidurals have several side effects, medical procedures are used to keep you and your baby safe. This is what you should expect when you have an epidural:

- Before an epidural, IV fluids are given to reduce the chance of a drop in blood pressure. This also allows other drugs to be given easily, if needed.

- Your blood pressure and pulse are checked frequently. If your blood pressure drops, you'll receive a medicine in your IV fluids to raise it. You may get an oxygen mask, too.

- You'll have an electronic monitor on your belly until your baby is born. This will check your labor contractions and your baby's heart rate. If contractions slow down, your nurse may give you medicine (*Pitocin*) to increase them. If your caregivers are concerned about your baby's heart rate, other procedures may be done.

- A clip is put on your finger to check your blood oxygen levels. If they're low, you'll be given an oxygen mask.

- Usually a *catheter* (small tube) is put into your bladder to help drain your pee.

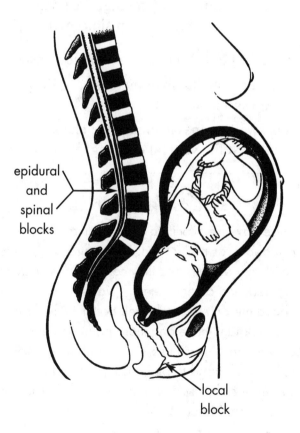

epidural and spinal blocks

local block

Local Anesthesia

Local anesthetics are used to numb the area around your vagina. Almost none of the medicine goes to your baby.

How Is Local Anesthesia Given?

You get a shot in the area around your vagina when it's time to push your baby down the birth canal.

How Does Local Anesthesia Help You?

- Local anesthesia gives good pain relief at the time of birth.
- It may be given before birth for an episiotomy or after the birth for stitching. (See page 151 for more information on episiotomy.)

What Are the Side Effects of Local Anesthesia?

- A local anesthetic may increase swelling in the vaginal area.
- This swelling may increase the chance of a tear at the vaginal opening.

❧ Cami's Story ❧

The nurse gave me Pitocin to get my contractions going, but my labor was really hard. The contractions were long and very painful. And they came so close together. When I reached 6 centimeters, I was exhausted. So, they gave me an epidural. I felt better immediately after that. I didn't have any more pain, so being stuck in bed with an IV wasn't so bad. Pushing was still hard work, but it felt good to being doing something. My friend Jenny didn't want an epidural for her labor, but I was glad I had one.

Ways to Reduce the Amount of Pain Medicine Used during Labor

If you don't want to use a lot of pain medicine during labor, here are some things you can do:

- Take childbirth classes and read this book to learn ways to reduce pain without taking medicines. Practice the labor-coping skills so you can use them easily. Also, learn about your medicine choices and how those drugs affect you and your baby.

- Have a birth partner or doula (or both) to help you with labor-coping skills.

- Before labor begins, choose the type of pain relief you'll want, if needed. Talk to your caregiver about your plans. Write your wishes in your birth plan.

- Make sure you and your partner know how to tell if you're coping well with labor. Can you keep a rhythm with your breathing or movement for a whole contraction? Can you relax between contractions? If so, you're coping well.

- If you feel like you're not coping well, try another breathing pattern. Have your partner help you maintain your rhythm. Then see how you do during the next 3 contractions. If you're still having difficulties, think about pain medicine.

- When you start thinking about having pain medicine, ask these questions: How far dilated am I? Is labor likely to last much longer? The answers may help you with your decision.

- If you decide to have medicine, ask for a low dose of the drug at first. Use more only if needed.

- Use the labor-coping skills for as long as possible.

- When you go to the hospital, ask for a nurse who enjoys caring for women having natural childbirth.

Helpful Hints on Handling Labor Pain

You should learn about all the pain relief methods during your pregnancy. This is especially important if you're planning not to use pain medicines during labor. However, you don't have to decide about using medicine until you're in labor. Try to make your decision by seeing how much pain you have—not by your fear of pain.

You'll probably start using relaxation and breathing patterns to help with the pain of early labor. As labor goes on, you'll add comfort measures to help you cope. Then you'll try other breathing patterns and coping skills in active labor. If you're coping well with the contractions, you won't need pain medicine. You can continue using the self-help skills.

If you feel that the pain is too intense, ask about pain medicines. Find out what you can use at this time in your labor. Ask about possible side effects. Then make your decision about medicine for pain relief.

CHAPTER 7

Challenging Labors and Cesarean Birth

You can't know beforehand what your labor will be like. If labor goes slower than expected, you may get very tired and discouraged. If it's faster than usual, labor contractions may be hard to handle. Having back pain in labor is also challenging. (For ways to cope with back pain, see pages 128–130.) It helps to know what you can do to keep labor and birth as normal as possible. This chapter describes different types of labors and births, including cesarean birth. It also tells you some ways to make these challenging births easier.

Starting Labor When It Doesn't Start on Its Own

Sometimes labor is slow to begin. You may go past your due date. Or you may have a long prelabor with days of contractions before your cervix begins to open. Occasionally, a doctor or midwife suggests starting labor before it starts on its own. *Inducing labor* or *induction* are terms used to describe starting labor with medical methods instead of letting it start on its own. If an induction is suggested, make sure you know the reason before agreeing to have it.

There should be a medical reason for inducing labor, such as protecting your health or keeping your baby safe. It isn't a good idea to start labor just because it would be more convenient. For example, don't start labor because you're tired of being pregnant. In that case, induction might cause more harm than good.

❧ Jenny's Story ❧

I thought my labor would never get going. The contractions started on a Monday. We went to the hospital, but they sent me home. The nurse said my contractions weren't strong enough and were too far apart. We went in 1 more time, and they gave me a sleeping pill. I didn't know what was wrong because I was in major pain. They said it was "false labor." There was nothing false about those contractions.
I just hung out at my mom's place. We went for walks and watched some TV. The pill did help me get a little sleep. My friend came over and told me stories that were a lot worse than what I was going through. On Wednesday, I went back to the hospital. I was finally in true labor and I got to stay.

What You Can Do When Labor Is Slow to Start

If you've gone past your due date, you may want to try the following methods to start labor. They may not work as quickly as medical methods, but some women try them first. Because some of these methods have side effects, talk to your caregiver before trying them.

Brisk walking may help start "true labor" when you're having prelabor contractions. However, walking is better at keeping labor going than starting it.

Castor oil is a strong laxative that women once used to start labor. Because it may cause painful cramping and diarrhea, not many women choose it now. If you're interested, ask your doctor or midwife about how to take it.

Sex causes contractions of the uterus, especially when you have an orgasm. When you're close to your due date, sex may start labor contractions. Also, semen has a substance in it called *prostaglandin*, which is the same thing your body makes to soften your cervix. When semen goes into your vagina during intercourse, the prostaglandin can help start labor. If you choose to have sex, try to make it as pleasant as possible. Think of it as a loving way to be with your partner. But *don't have sex if your bag of waters has broken.*

Rubbing your nipples lightly makes you produce more *oxytocin* (the hormone that causes your uterus to contract). This method, called *nipple stimulation*, may help to start labor. Remember to tell your caregiver if you plan to use this method because it sometimes causes contractions that last too long or come too close together. So, *stop rubbing your nipples as soon as labor begins.* That means: Stop if contractions become painful, last longer than 1 minute, or come every 5 minutes or less.

You can lightly stroke or rub a nipple with your fingertips or a soft washcloth. Or you can roll the nipple between your fingers. Within a few minutes, you may feel uterine contractions. If not, try rubbing both nipples. Because contractions may stop when you stop stroking, you may want to do it on and off for several hours. Stroking and nipple rolling should be gentle and light. Don't rub so hard that your nipples get sore.

Medical Methods to Start Labor

There are several methods doctors and midwives use to induce labor. Here are the most common ones:

Prostaglandin is put into the vagina to help ripen (soften) the cervix. The drug is the same as the prostaglandin made by your body. It comes in different forms—as a gel, a tampon-like device, or a capsule or pill. Prostaglandin is often used before Pitocin is started to make the cervix more ready to open with the contractions. A nurse usually watches you closely for at least 2 hours after this method is used.

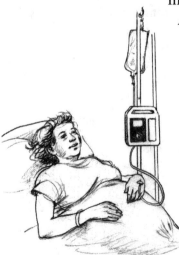

Pitocin (a drug that's just like the oxytocin made by your body) is given to cause the uterus to contract. Pitocin is given by an IV drip at the hospital. The nurse usually starts at a low dose and steadily increases it. The goal is to have contractions that are similar to those in active labor.

Starting labor with Pitocin can be more stressful than allowing labor to start normally. It may take several hours before contractions start. But when they do, they may be close together and painful. These contractions can be hard to handle and emotionally draining.

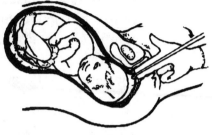

Artificial rupture of the membranes (*AROM*) means breaking the bag of waters with a plastic *amnihook*. This method may be used to start labor, but it's used more often during labor to help speed up labor progress.

❧ Cami's Story ❧

My blood pressure went up and my doctor wanted to start labor. I was okay with that. It took a long time though. First, they used the gel because my cervix wasn't ready to open. Then they gave me Pitocin in an IV. Later they broke my bag of waters. That didn't hurt, but it felt like I'd peed in the bed. I felt bad about soaking the bed, but the nurse didn't make a big deal about it.

Then I waited. Jeff and I played cards and watched TV. When I told Jeff to turn off the TV, he said, "Can't we wait till the show's over?" I yelled, "Turn it off NOW!" I didn't want any noise. It was all I could do to deal with the strong pains. The contractions came one after another and I had trouble coping with them. I was lucky that my blood pressure was okay through all that.

Short, Fast Labor

Though a short labor may sound good, it's often overwhelming. When labor lasts less than 3 hours, the early phase has usually passed unnoticed. Then you find yourself in active, hard labor and feel unprepared for the painful contractions. Your partner may be surprised at your reaction to what is supposed to be early labor. Do your best to tell your partner and your nurse how they can help you.

What You Can Do If You're in Very Hard Labor

- Don't give up on yourself. Trust your ability to get through this.

- Quickly go to the hospital or birth center.

- Try not to tense up with painful contractions. Instead, try to relax as much as possible.

- Try slow breathing to help you relax during contractions. If that doesn't help, try light breathing.

- You'll need help from your partner, nurse, or doula in handling the painful contractions. In a fast labor, your contractions will be intense and very effective.

- Have a vaginal exam before you make any decision about pain medicines. If you're very close to having your baby, you may decide not to have any medicine.

- You may have the urge to push before your caregiver is ready. If this happens, lie on your side rather than using an upright position, and pant. Or only bear down gently.

- After the birth, you'll probably feel relieved but stunned that labor is over so quickly. If you can't remember much about your birth, talk to your partner or caregivers. They can share their memories with you.

What If Your Baby Is Born Before You Get to the Hospital?

Sometimes labor is so fast that you can't get to the hospital in time. Or your midwife arrives late for a home birth. When this happens, babies are born without medical care. Luckily, this doesn't happen very often.

If your baby is really ready to be born or is coming out, it's better to stay at home than to try to get to the hospital. If your baby starts to come out while you're in the car, stop at the side of the road. Then, after your baby is born, continue on to the hospital.

How Will You Know That Your Baby Is Really Coming?

- You'll feel your body pushing (holding your breath and straining) and you won't be able to stop it.
- You'll see or touch your baby's head at the vaginal opening.
- You'll feel your baby coming out.

Usually babies born fast are healthy. However, the following checklist will help you have the best possible outcome during such an emergency. You may want to keep it handy in case you need it at home or on your way to the hospital.

Quick Checklist for Birth without Medical Help

Follow these steps if you're alone. (Or do as many as you can.) If you have a partner or helper, then this person can help you as needed.

1. Get help, if possible. Call your partner, the hospital, and/or 911.
2. Gather clean sheets, towels, or extra clothing.

3. Wash your hands, if possible.

4. Put a sheet, towel, or some clothing under your bare bottom.

5. Lie down on your side or sit leaning back. Make sure you have enough room for your baby to lie down when she slips out of the birth canal.

6. Pant through each contraction until your baby is born. Try not to hold your breath even though you feel like pushing.

7. After your baby comes out:
   - Wipe away the mucus from her nose and mouth.
   - Dry her head and body.
   - Place her on your bare chest or belly.
   - Keep her warm using a blanket, towel, or piece of clothing.

9. Do not cut the cord. Let your baby nuzzle or suckle on your breast. Or breastfeed your baby, if possible.

10. After the placenta comes out, place it near your baby (still attached by the cord) in a bowl, newspaper, or cloth.

11. Place towels or a pad between your legs to soak up the blood flow.

12. Get medical help as soon as possible to check both you and your baby.
   - If you're at home, wait until the placenta is delivered before having someone take you and your baby to the hospital. Call the hospital to let them know you're coming.

     If you've waited for more than 30 minutes and the placenta hasn't come out, call the hospital and ask the nurses what to do. Then go to the hospital.

- If you had planned a home birth, call your midwife so she can come and check on you and your baby.

Long, Slow Labor

Long, drawn-out labors are more common than fast ones, especially if this is your first baby. Your labor could be very slow only during early labor, or only during active labor, or both. If you have a long labor, you may become discouraged and very tired.

Long Early Labor

If you're having a long early phase, it doesn't mean that the rest of your labor will be extra long. In most cases, labor progresses normally once you reach the active phase. In addition, a long prelabor or early phase (1–3 centimeters dilation) is not usually caused by a medical problem.

What You Can Do for a Long Early Labor

It's easier to get through a long, slow labor if you know what's happening. It also helps to know that you have some choices:

- If you have a vaginal exam during your visit with your caregiver, ask questions. Find out if your cervix is soft. Ask how much your cervix has thinned. Find out how far you're dilated. Remember that your cervix needs to be soft and thin before it begins to open.

- Time some of your contractions while you're at home. (See pages 79–80.) Time 4 or 5 contractions in a row. Then wait a few hours (or until your labor pattern changes) before timing some more.

- Try not to become discouraged or depressed. Take care of yourself. Eat and drink, but stay away from greasy foods.

- Do whatever sounds good to you. Think of something to help keep your mind off the contractions. Try taking a walk, watching a movie, going shopping, or cooking.

- Also, try to rest. You probably won't be able to sleep. (If you could, there wouldn't be a problem!) If you are very tired, a warm bath may slow your contractions and let you get more rest.

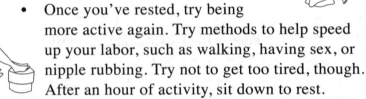

- Once you've rested, try being more active again. Try methods to help speed up your labor, such as walking, having sex, or nipple rubbing. Try not to get too tired, though. After an hour of activity, sit down to rest.

- If you're worried during early labor, try to have kind, supportive people around you (family members, friends, a doula, or nurses). Emotional stress (anger, worry, tension) sometimes slows labor progress. Try using relaxation techniques and slow breathing to feel calmer and ease the pain.

Medical Care during a Long Early Labor

If your contractions tire you out or if it takes more than 24 hours to get to 3 centimeters dilation, your caregiver may suggest one or both of these medical methods to help you:

1. Drugs to try to stop the contractions and give you time to rest, such as:

    - A sleeping pill

- A narcotic pill or shot, such as morphine
2. Ways to make your contractions more effective, such as:
   - Breaking your bag of waters
   - Ripening your cervix with prostaglandin
   - Inducing labor with Pitocin

Long Active Labor

Usually active labor moves along quickly. After you reach 4 centimeters dilation, your cervix normally dilates 1 centimeter every hour or so. Problems are more likely if labor slows or stops when you're in active labor. If you go for several hours with no change in dilation, your doctor or midwife will watch you and the baby more closely while trying methods to speed up labor. This will help keep you and your baby safe.

What You Can Do for a Long Active Labor

The solution will depend on the problem. Here are possible causes and ways to encourage labor progress in active labor:

- If you have a full bladder, go to the bathroom. Try to pee every hour to give more space for your baby to pass through your pelvis.
- If you've been in bed for 30 minutes or more, try walking, swaying, or standing.
- If you need to stay in bed, change positions about every 30 minutes. Try lying on one side or another, sitting up in bed, or getting on your hands and knees.

- If your contractions are far apart or weak, try nipple rubbing or walking.

- If you're anxious, talk about your fears. Fear increases pain and can slow labor.

- If you're tense, try comfort measures such as a bath, massage, or shower.

- If the pain is too much for you and you can't handle it with what you're doing, try other breathing and relaxation techniques.

- If you're discouraged, you'll need encouragement and support from your labor partner and nurse.

Medical Care When Active Labor Is Very Slow

Keeping your baby safe is the focus of medical care when labor is slow. During a long active phase, your caregiver will also pay close attention to your labor progress.

- You'll probably have vaginal exams to check for cervical dilation and the baby's movement down the birth canal.

- Your baby's health will also be closely watched. Your caregiver will check your baby's heart rate frequently, probably with the electronic fetal monitor rather than the Doppler.

- If your baby's heart rate shows problems, it may mean that your baby is pressing on his cord and needs more oxygen. Your caregiver will try something to fix the problem, such as:

* Having you roll over or get on your hands and knees

* Helping to put water back into your uterus to replace the water that came out when your bag of waters broke

* Giving you an oxygen mask, which gives you and your baby more oxygen

- You're likely to have IV fluids to make sure you don't lose too much water from your body from sweating, peeing, or vomiting. You need plenty of water and it's sometimes hard to drink enough during labor.

- You may have (and want) medicines for relaxation and pain relief if your labor is very long.

- Your caregiver may break your bag of waters to help speed up your labor.

- Also, you may be given Pitocin to make your contractions stronger and closer together. If you were planning a home birth, you'll go to the hospital if you need Pitocin.

- If labor does not progress, even with Pitocin, a cesarean birth may be necessary.

Long Second Stage

When the second stage of labor is long, you may need medical help to push the baby out. Sometimes a caregiver does an episiotomy to make the vaginal opening larger and shorten the pushing time. An *episiotomy* is a cut made with scissors from your vagina toward your rectum. After the birth, this cut is closed with stitches.

Other medical procedures may also be used. A *vacuum extractor* (plastic suction cup) or *forceps* (metal tongs) may be used to help deliver your baby's head. During a contraction, while you push, the doctor pulls with the vacuum or forceps to help your baby come down. These methods are generally safe for the baby, but they may cause bruises or sore spots on your baby's head.

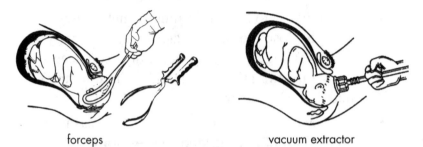

forceps   vacuum extractor

It helps to know about these procedures before birth. Plan to talk to your caregiver about them. If you have any concerns or choices about these procedures, write them in your birth plan. Then you'll be prepared if they're suggested during birth.

Cesarean Birth

A *cesarean birth* is the surgical delivery of your baby through an incision in your lower belly and uterus. This is also called a *cesarean section* or *C-section*. Because cesarean birth is major surgery, it's usually done only if there's a medical reason. If there's no medical reason for a cesarean, a vaginal birth is usually safer for both you and your baby.

If you have a cesarean birth, you have fewer choices, but you still have some. As you read this section, think about what you would choose if a cesarean birth became necessary. Then write down your choices in your birth plan. This may help you feel better and more in control if you do need a cesarean.

Reasons for Having a Cesarean Birth

Sometimes the need for a cesarean is known before labor begins. Other times a cesarean is done because of problems that come up during labor. Here are the main reasons for having a cesarean.

Reasons That Are Usually Known before Labor Begins

1. There are problems with the placenta.
    (See pages 32–33.)

    *   If the placenta is covering the cervix (*placenta previa*), the placenta would come out before the baby. So, a safe vaginal birth isn't possible.

    *   If the placenta has separated from the uterus (*placental abruption*), the baby is getting less oxygen. A cesarean may be necessary.

2. The mother has medical problems that make vaginal birth unsafe.

    *   If you have heart disease, the stress of labor may be too much for you.

    *   If you have an active genital herpes infection, your baby may get the infection when going through the birth canal.

    *   If you're HIV positive, your baby is less likely to get the virus if you have a planned cesarean.

3. The baby has a birth defect that would be made worse with a vaginal birth.

Reasons That Occur during Labor

1. Active labor is very slow and isn't progressing. This means the cervix isn't opening well or the baby isn't coming down through the pelvis or birth canal. Since early labor (0–4 centimeters

dilation) is usually slow, it's a problem only when labor slows down after 5 centimeters dilation.

2. The baby is in a poor position for a vaginal birth.

- If the baby were coming bottom first or feet first (*breech*), there may be problems with a vaginal birth. Only 3–4 babies out of every 100 are breech.

- If the baby is lying sideways or the baby's face (instead of the top of the baby's head) is coming first, a vaginal birth is unsafe. These positions are rare.

- Sometimes the baby's head is down, but it's facing the wrong way or is tilted to 1 side. These positions make it harder for the baby to come down the birth canal.

3. The baby isn't coming down into the pelvis. This doesn't usually mean the baby's head is too big or the baby weighs too much. It often means the baby's head is tilted or turned in such a way that it doesn't fit through your pelvis.

4. The baby is having trouble handling the stress of labor (called *fetal distress*). Certain changes in the baby's heart rate during labor show that the baby may not be getting enough oxygen.

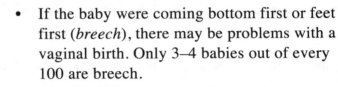

5. The umbilical cord is coming through the cervix before the baby (*prolapsed cord*). When the cord comes first, labor contractions press the baby onto the cord. This means the baby gets less oxygen during a contraction. A prolapsed cord rarely occurs when a baby's head is down against the cervix.

6. The mother had a cesarean birth before. Sometimes a doctor suggests a *repeat cesarean birth*. However, many women don't want another cesarean if it isn't needed. Taking care of a new baby and an older child is harder after surgery. A safe vaginal birth is possible after a previous cesarean. It's called a *vaginal birth after cesarean* (*VBAC*). However, another cesarean may be done if the same problem that caused the first cesarean still exists.

✦ Cami's Story ✦

The cesarean came as a big surprise. I mean, even though my labor took a long time to get started, I moved along when I got to hard labor. Then when it was time to push, I was happy. I thought I'd be seeing little Tommy soon. Well, I pushed and pushed for I don't know how long. The nurse kept checking me while I pushed—putting her fingers inside me to feel the baby's head. After a while, the doctor did the same thing. He said the baby was stuck and wasn't coming down. He was real nice when he said, "You've worked so hard and done a good job. But we have to do something else. For your baby's safety, we should do a cesarean." I couldn't believe it! How could I be so close and not get my baby out? I cried. But I knew they were right. So, I said, "Okay. At least labor will be over soon."

Side Effects of a Cesarean Birth

A cesarean birth is the safest option when certain problems arise. Some women think it would be quicker and easier to have a cesarean even if there aren't problems. But a cesarean isn't as easy on the mother and baby as you might think. When you and your baby are healthy, a vaginal birth is the best choice. To learn more about the benefits and risks of cesarean birth, talk to your caregiver.

These are some possible risks of having a cesarean birth:

- Problems related to the anesthesia used for surgery
- Pain for several weeks after the birth
- Greater risk of infection and blood loss than with a vaginal birth
- Harder time taking care of your baby
- More problems with a future pregnancy (including problems getting pregnant again and having a healthy placenta)
- Increased risk of cesarean for the next birth

What Happens during a Cesarean?

Before the cesarean birth, your nurse will explain what happens during the operation. You'll be asked to sign a consent form giving your permission for surgery. Make sure you understand the reasons for and the risks of the cesarean before signing the form.

The nurse will start an IV in your lower arm or hand. She'll shave your belly about 2 inches above and 2 inches below where the incision will be. You'll be given an antacid to drink to reduce the acid in your stomach. A fetal monitor will be placed on your belly to check on your baby.

Next, you'll be moved to the surgery room. Once you're in the operating room, the *anesthesiologist* (a doctor who gives anesthesia) will talk with you about the medicines. Then you'll be given anesthesia. Usually spinal or epidural anesthesia is used because it allows you to be awake without feeling pain. The anesthesia numbs you from your lower chest to your feet.

Nausea, shaking or trembling, and a drop in blood pressure often happen with epidural and spinal anesthesia. Make sure to tell your caregivers if you're feeling pain or are having trouble breathing. Also, they want to know if you're feeling uncomfortable, nauseated, cold, or afraid. They can help you feel better.

The nurse will put a small tube (*catheter*) into your bladder to keep it empty. Usually the nurse waits to insert the catheter until after the anesthetic has taken effect so you won't feel it. The IV and catheter are removed within 24 hours after the surgery.

During the surgery, you lie on your back tilted a bit to 1 side. The nurse washes your belly with an antiseptic (a germ-fighting soap). Then a surgical sheet with a hole near your belly is put over your body. Also, a sheet or drape is hung between your head and belly. This keeps the surgical area clean and may keep you from seeing the surgery. Your partner usually stands or sits near your head. In this position, he or she can hold your hand, talk to you, and help you use slow breathing to remain calm.

✨ *Cami's Story* ✨

I was scared, but the cesarean wasn't so bad. Jeff was with me. He held my hand, but he was nervous and didn't say much. There were a lot of people there—3 doctors and a bunch of nurses. It was cold in the room and I had the shakes. The anesthesia doctor talked to me and gave me something to stop my shaking. I could feel some pushing and pulling in my belly, but it didn't really hurt.

I couldn't believe how quickly the baby came out! It seemed like they had just started when I heard him cry. Then I cried. I thanked everybody in the room. Jeff even cried.

You may be surprised at all the people and equipment needed for a cesarean delivery. Besides you and your partner, there are several others:

- 2 doctors who do the surgery (a certified nurse midwife can replace 1 of the doctors)
- An anesthesiologist
- 1 or 2 nurses
- Sometimes another doctor or nurse to care for your baby

There are several ways to check on your safety during the surgery:

- A blood pressure cuff on your arm
- Heart rate monitors on your chest
- A soft clip on your finger

A cesarean takes about 45 minutes to 1 hour. However, the baby is usually born 10–15 minute after surgery begins. During a cesarean, the doctor makes 2 incisions: 1 through your skin and the other through your uterus. Your abdominal muscles aren't cut; they're spread apart. You probably won't feel any pain during the surgery. But you may feel some pressure, tugging, and pulling.

The doctor takes your baby out and suctions mucus and fluid from his nose and mouth. The doctor cuts and clamps the cord and gives you a quick look at your baby. Your baby is then placed on a warm bed. The nurse dries him and makes sure he's doing well. Then your baby is wrapped in a warm blanket.

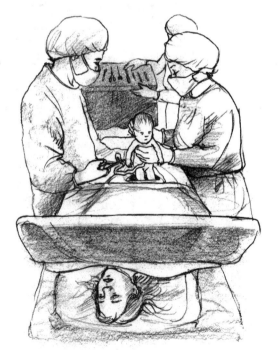

Incision for a cesarean birth

As long as your baby is healthy, your partner can hold him close to you or put him on your chest. If your arms are strapped down, ask about having an arm free. You may enjoy seeing and touching your baby while the doctor is finishing the operation.

After the birth, Pitocin is usually added to your IV to make your uterus contract to prevent heavy bleeding. When your doctor is removing your placenta, you may feel some pressure or tugging. It takes about 30 minutes for the doctor to close the incisions in your uterus and belly. A thick pressure bandage will be placed over your incision.

Cami's Story

The cesarean wasn't over when the baby came out. They still had to sew me up. I got the shakes again and felt sick to my stomach. The doctor told me that this was common with cesareans. He said to take a few deep breaths and breathe through my mouth. He also put a warm blanket on my chest. I had a pain in my shoulder. It didn't help to have Jeff rub it. The doctor said the pain came from having air inside my belly and that it would go away in awhile.

At least I could see Tommy while they were sewing me up. They sucked the mucus out of his nose and mouth and he cried real loud. Then they gave him some oxygen to breathe. When they were done, Jeff got to hold him. Then Jeff brought him over to me and I said, "Hi, Tommy" and kissed him. My beautiful baby made everything okay.

The First Hours after a Cesarean Birth (Recovery)

During the first hours after a cesarean, you'll be in your hospital room or in a special recovery room. The nurse checks your blood pressure, your incision, and the amount of vaginal bleeding on your pad. You'll be watched closely until the anesthesia wears off (2–4 hours). Your baby will also be checked often. As long as your baby is doing well, he may stay with you. Although you may be groggy, you'll be able to hold and admire him. You'll also be able to breastfeed at this time. Be sure to ask for help if you need it.

Pain Relief after a Cesarean Birth

The first few days after a cesarean are the most difficult. Pain in your incision will probably bother you quite a lot at first, but it will gradually decrease. You may need pain medicine for several days to a week. You might wonder if it's safe for your baby to get strong pain medicine while you're breastfeeding. Only a small amount goes to your baby through your breast milk. So, it's still better to breastfeed your baby. It's a good idea to use enough pain medicine to allow you to care for yourself and your baby.

There are 2 common ways to treat your pain during the first day after surgery:

- One method is to have narcotic medicine put into the epidural or spinal catheter while you're in the operating room. This gives you good pain relief for about 24 hours and doesn't make you sleepy or drowsy. However, itching and nausea are possible side effects. Your nurse can give you other medicine to decrease the itching and nausea, but it might make you sleepy.

- Another method is called *patient-controlled analgesia* (*PCA*). With PCA, a narcotic goes into the fluid in your IV tubing. Whenever you need pain relief, you press a button to get a small dose of the narcotic. The PCA machine is set up to give only the dose ordered by the doctor (and only as often as it's safe). This provides faster pain relief than if you had to ask a nurse for a pain shot. However, IV narcotics may make you sleepy.

After the first day, most mothers use pain pills. At first, they contain narcotics. Later, they contain only a mild pain medicine such as acetaminophen (Tylenol) or ibuprofen. The dose depends on the mother's pain and her need to take care of herself and her baby. After a cesarean birth, taking pain pills may make it easier for you to move around, feed, and care for your baby. When the pain is gone, stop using them—even if you haven't used all of them.

Recovery from a Cesarean Birth

In the first days after a cesarean, you'll need help doing almost everything. Your incision will hurt and it'll be hard to move around. Your partner may be able to stay in your hospital room to help with baby care. If your partner can't stay, the nurse will help you as you recover from surgery.

Here are a few ways to be more comfortable during the early days of your recovery:

Rolling over: To make rolling from your back to your side easier and less painful, try this method (called *bridging*):

1. Bend your knees 1 leg at a time so your feet are flat on the bed.

2. Lift your hips while keeping your feet and shoulders on the bed.

3. Keep your body straight from shoulders to knees. Then twist your hips to 1 side while rolling your shoulders to the same side.

4. Now you're lying on your side.

Standing and walking: When you first get out of bed after a cesarean, your nurse will help you. You'll probably feel weak, dizzy, and a little lightheaded. Try these things to reduce the dizziness:

- Sit on the edge of the bed and move your feet in circles (before standing up).

- Slowly stand up. Try to stand as straight as you can. It won't harm your incision even though it hurts.

- Take a short walk after you get used to standing up.

- Take a slightly longer walk each time you get out of bed.

Going to the bathroom: Your first time out of bed may be a trip to the bathroom. Sometimes it's difficult to pee after having a catheter in your bladder. If you have trouble, try these things:

- Pour warm water near your vagina to help start the flow

- Pee in the shower or tub

- Cough to help start the flow while sitting on the toilet (If coughing makes your incision hurt, gently press against your incision with your hand or a small towel.)

Dealing with gas pains in your belly: Having a cesarean or any abdominal surgery can cause gas in your stomach and bowels. After the surgery, your belly hurts as gas moves through your bowels. If you have gas pains, getting in and out of bed helps pass the gas. Walking or rocking in a chair helps, too. Avoid eating foods that cause gas.

Home after a Cesarean

You'll stay in the hospital 2–4 days. You won't be back to normal by then, however. You'll still be sore, weak, and tired. It takes time to recover from a cesarean birth. If possible, try to have help at home for the first few weeks. You'll feel better sooner if you have help with meals, baby care, and housework.

After a cesarean birth, you may feel relieved and thankful. Or you may feel sad, disappointed, or angry instead of happy and joyful as you expected. If you have trouble adjusting emotionally to your cesarean, talk with your partner or caregiver. You may want to be told again why the cesarean was necessary. Or you may just want to talk honestly and openly about the birth and your feelings. Talking with others may help you overcome your feelings of anger or sadness.

Conclusion

Labor and birth happen in many different ways. No one knows ahead of time if childbirth will be fast or slow or have problems or not. You usually don't know whether your baby will be fine or have a health problem. By knowing about the many differences in labors and births, it'll be easier to cope with what happens.

CHAPTER 8

Home with Your New Baby: Now You're a Mom

Having a baby begins a new phase in your life—becoming a parent. This chapter describes what it's like to be a new mother in the first few weeks and months after birth. These early months are called the *postpartum period*.

Going Home

Most new mothers leave the hospital about 1 or 2 days after the birth. If you have a cesarean birth, you can expect to stay about 2–4 days. If either you or your baby needs more medical attention, you may stay longer. If you have your baby at an out-of-hospital birth center, you'll go home 3–6 hours after the birth. With a home birth, the midwife usually leaves 3 or 4 hours after the birth.

Plan to have loose, comfortable clothes to wear when you go home. You probably won't fit into the pants you wore before pregnancy. You can wear either your maternity clothes or some stretchy, larger clothes. The hospital will put a clean diaper on your baby before you leave. So, remember to bring baby clothes. (See the packing list on pages 70–71.)

If you're going home in a car, you'll need an infant car seat. Put it in your car before your baby's born. Make sure you know how to install the car seat correctly. Sometimes it's hard to get it in just right. If you aren't sure how it fits in your car, ask your caregiver about ways to get help. Some hospitals have classes on buying and installing car seats. (See page 245 for more on car safety.) If you don't have the money to buy a car seat, ask your caregiver or social worker how to get a low-cost or free one.

Caring for Yourself

After having your baby, you'll look and feel very different than before you were pregnant. By 6 weeks after birth, you'll probably start feeling "normal" again. It may take a little longer to get back to your old size and shape.

What to Expect in Your Changing Body

These are some of the normal physical changes in the first weeks after the birth.

Your Uterus

When you're not pregnant, your uterus is about the size of a pear. Right after the birth, it's about the size of a large grapefruit (and feels like one, too). It stays about that size for the next few days. Mild uterine contractions keep it firm and tight. If you touch your belly near your bellybutton, you can feel the top of your uterus. When

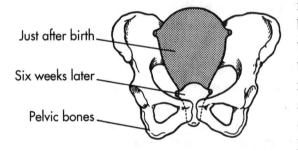

Just after birth

Six weeks later

Pelvic bones

it's hard, it helps stop bleeding from the area where the placenta used to be. When it relaxes, it feels softer and you may bleed more. (Breastfeeding is very helpful in keeping your uterus firm.) Gradually, your uterus gets smaller. After 5 or 6 weeks, it's almost back to its usual size.

After birth, you'll have a lot of vaginal bleeding (called *lochia*). You'll need to wear a big pad instead of a small one. You shouldn't use a tampon in the first weeks after the birth. Your flow will be like a heavy period. It's normal to pass soft blood clots (like jelly), especially in the first days after the birth.

At certain times you may notice more clots or blood. But this doesn't mean that you're bleeding more. The blood that was already in your uterus is just coming out. Your flow is heavier:

- When you stand up after you've been lying down
- When you have a bowel movement
- As you breastfeed

After 1 or 2 weeks, your vaginal bleeding slows down and becomes a lighter color. It gradually changes from red to pink and then to tan or yellow. Your flow usually goes away after about 6 weeks or so. But if it increases or returns to bright red, call your caregiver.

Afterpains are strong cramps in your uterus after the birth. They're stronger during the first days if you're breastfeeding. Also, they're more common if you've had a baby before. Afterpains feel like strong menstrual cramps. To reduce the pain, try using the slow breathing you learned for labor (or anything you did for cramps during your periods). If needed, ask your doctor or midwife for some pain pills. Afterpains usually go away after the first week or so.

Menstrual periods begin again about 4–8 weeks after the birth if you're not breastfeeding. If you're breastfeeding, you may not have a period until you start giving your baby other foods. Some breastfeeding mothers start their periods within a few months after giving birth, though this isn't common. And some don't have a period until they stop breastfeeding.

You can get pregnant even if you haven't had a period yet. If you don't want to get pregnant soon after the birth, use birth control when you have sex. (See pages 186–187 for more on family planning.)

Your Birth Canal (Vagina and Perineum)

Your vagina slowly but surely goes back to the way it was before the birth. Expect some pain if you've had stitches or if the vaginal area is bruised. Your stitches *dissolve* (go away) on their own in a few weeks, so they don't need to be removed. The pain from bruising or stitches usually goes away in 4–6 weeks or by the time you heal.

Here are a few suggestions to help with healing and to reduce pain near the birth canal:

- Put an ice pack on your perineum (the vaginal area). After birth, the nurse will do this for you. At home, put crushed ice or a frozen wet washcloth in a zip-lock bag and wrap it in paper towels. Hold it in place on your perineum with your pad. Do this for 20 minutes, then take it off. Try to do it 2 or 3 times each day during the first few days.

- After you pee, clean yourself by pouring warm water over your perineum while you're sitting on the toilet. Or use a *peri bottle* (a squeeze bottle they give you at the hospital) to squirt the water on your bottom. Pat or wipe yourself dry from front to back. Wiping from front to back helps prevent infection from germs in the area where you have bowel movements.

- Begin doing some Kegel exercises soon after the birth. (See page 43.) Don't be discouraged if you can't do them as well as you could before the birth. The strength of your pelvic floor muscles will improve over time.

- *Witch hazel* pads may provide soothing pain relief for stitches and hemorrhoids. Lay them on your pad before you put it on. Witch hazel pads (like Tucks) can be purchased from a drugstore. Or you can buy a bottle of witch hazel and pour some onto a few small pads. Then freeze them. Place a fresh homemade moist pad onto your larger pad each time you change it.

- Take a *sitz bath*. Sit in a clean tub of warm water for 10–20 minutes. You need only enough water to cover your bottom—a full tub isn't necessary. Then get out, dry off, and lie down for 15 minutes. Lying down after your bath helps reduce the swelling in the area around your vagina. Take a sitz bath 2–4 times a day until your bottom feels better.

- Lie down and rest as often as you can in the first week or two after the birth. When you sit or stand for a long time, it increases the swelling and pain around your vagina.

✍ *Maria's Story* ✍

Sitting down really hurt because I had stitches and my bottom was sore. The thing that helped me most was sitting in the tub with a little warm water. I also tried to lie down most of the time in the first few days. The pain pills they gave me in the hospital helped me when I started standing up more.

Your Breasts

For breastfeeding mothers. For 2 or 3 days after the birth, your breasts will produce special milk called *colostrum*. This is the only food your baby needs for the first few days after birth. Then your milk supply will increase quickly. Most mothers say their milk "came in" when their breasts became full and hard. When you make more milk, your breasts usually get bigger. Let your baby nurse often or at least every 2–3 hours. This decreases the fullness and helps prevent your breasts from getting too painful. (See Chapter 9 for more on breastfeeding.)

For mothers who don't breastfeed. Your breasts will probably go through the same changes as a breastfeeding mother at first. You may have a few days of heaviness and pain in your breasts. Try these methods to make you more comfortable and to stop your breasts from making milk:

1. Bind your breasts with a wide elastic bandage (like an Ace bandage), a sports bra, or a very tight bra. Wear the bandage or bra for 1–2 days starting on the second or third day after the birth. Wear it all day long, even while sleeping.

2. Apply ice packs when your breasts begin to feel full and hard. Put an ice pack on top of the bandage or bra every 4 hours for 20 minutes during the daytime.

3. Do not breastfeed. And don't try to remove any milk from your breasts with a breast pump or by hand expression (squeezing milk out with your hand). This will cause your breasts to make even more milk.

4. Take ibuprofen as ordered by your doctor or midwife. This will decrease the swelling and pain.

In the past, women were given shots or pills to "dry up" their milk. These methods aren't available now because of their serious side effects. Also, they didn't work any better than the suggestions in this list.

Head-Lift Exercise

After pregnancy, some women notice a wide gap between their tummy muscles near their bellybutton. A small gap is normal between these muscles (the *rectus* muscles). Doing this exercise helps strengthen these muscles and bring them closer together.

1. Lie on your back with your knees bent.
2. Cross your arms over your belly.
   Put your hands beside your waist.
3. Breathe in.
4. As you breathe out, raise your head and shoulders. At the same time, pull your hands toward your bellybutton.
5. Hold for a slow count of 5.
6. Put your head down and rest for about 10 seconds.
7. Repeat about 10 times a day until the gap is smaller.

Your Muscles and Joints

After the birth, it takes about 6 weeks for your belly muscles to regain their strength and tone. Exercise helps speed up this process. (See page 171 and pages 180–181.) If you had a cesarean birth, your belly will be sore near the *incision* (the cut into your belly.). So, in the first week, do only mild exercises for your tummy muscles. Your doctor or midwife will tell you when you can return to regular exercise.

Some women feel pain in the tailbone, hips, pelvis, or lower back after the birth. Your tailbone may have been bruised when your baby came down the birth canal. If you pulled your legs very wide apart during birth, your hips may be sore for a while after the birth. If you have pain that makes it hard to walk, sit, or roll over, tell your caregiver.

Your Bladder and Bowels

You may have trouble peeing because your bottom may be sore or swollen. Usually this lasts only a few days.

You may also have trouble with bowel movements after the birth. If you had an episiotomy, you may have pain from a sore bottom. Also, iron pills or pain pills can make your bowel movements harder (*constipation*). Try these suggestions to help you have normal bowel movements:

- Take stool softeners. You may be given stool softeners at the hospital before you go home. You can buy stool softeners at a drugstore. If they're ordered by your doctor or midwife, your insurance may help pay for them.

- Eat foods with fiber such as fresh fruits, dried fruits, fresh vegetables, dark breads, cereal, beans, and lentils.

- Drink plenty of water.

- Walk and do exercises that tighten your belly muscles.

- Go to the bathroom when you feel the need to have a bowel movement. Don't wait.

- If these ideas don't help, talk to your caregiver about other medicines to relieve constipation.

Hemorrhoids (sometimes called *piles*) are painful, swollen veins in your rectum (where your poop comes out). They're common during pregnancy and more common right after birth. Hemorrhoids usually go away within a month or so after birth. Try these suggestions to decrease the pain and help hemorrhoids heal:

- Avoid constipation. Try to have regular bowel movements. Drink plenty of water and eat high-fiber foods. Take a stool softener each day if you need one.

- Try Kegel exercises. (See page 43). These tighten the muscles in the rectum, too.

- Use any method that worked for you during pregnancy or that you were told to try in the hospital.

- Talk to your doctor or midwife about medicines to relieve the discomfort of hemorrhoids.

Warning Signs during Post Partum

Some problems may come up after you get home. You may wonder if they're normal or serious. If you notice any of the following warning signs, call your caregiver right away:

- Fever (Your temperature, taken by mouth, goes up to 100.4°F or 38°C or higher.)
- Very heavy vaginal flow (enough to soak a big pad in an hour or less) and/or having a blood clot larger than a lemon in your flow
- Stinky smell from your vagina (could smell fishy) or vaginal soreness or itching
- More pain at the site of stitches than there was the day before
- Trouble peeing or pain when you pee
- Sore, red, hot area on your breast, along with fever
- Feeling very anxious, angry, sad, or panicky, along with trouble sleeping and eating
- Sore, red, painful area on your leg (It could be a dangerous blood clot.)
- Pain in the bone under your pubic hair or in your lower back, along with trouble walking
- If you had a cesarean, increased pain and redness around the incision, and/or pus running out of your scar
- Any new pain or sudden soreness or discomfort
- Fear of abuse or violence toward you or your baby by your partner or family member

Medical Care after the Birth

You should have a checkup once or twice during the first 2 months after your baby's born. Try to make an appointment soon after the birth. If you wait, your doctor or midwife may be too busy to see you for a long time. Your caregiver will check your physical recovery, perineum, stitches (if necessary), and vaginal flow. If you had a cesarean birth, your scar will be checked, too. Your caregiver may check your breasts and talk to you about breastfeeding. You'll also have a chance to talk about any physical or emotional problems. Talk to your caregiver about family planning. This is a good time to choose a birth control method if you haven't already.

A Reminder

Make sure to call your caregiver **right away** if you notice any of the warning signs on page 174. Don't wait for your next appointment.

Help and Support

As a new mother, you may be surprised at how hard it is to take care of a brand-new baby, especially if it's your first one. When you think about it, it's a big job. You're recovering from pregnancy and birth, and you have to learn this new job. In addition, you aren't getting a full night's sleep because your baby needs to eat and have her diapers changed.

It's normal to need some help when you have a new baby. If you have help, you'll get used to being a mother quicker. (It helps a new dad, too.) Also, you'll have more time to sleep and rest.

❧ Jenny's Story ❧

Mom wanted me to stay at her place after Emily was born, so she could take care of me. I think Kyle was glad. He had to go back to work right away, and he wanted me to have some help. I was pretty sore after the birth, especially my bottom and breasts. I spent most of the first week lying around holding my baby. Mom treated me like a princess. Kyle came over after work every day. He's great with Emily.

Try to say yes when people offer to help, if you think they'll be helpful. Most people are glad when you accept their help. Some people don't offer because they don't want to get in the way. So, make sure to ask for help if you need it. Maybe your mother, aunt, or sister can stay for a while. Friends from work, church members, or neighbors may be happy to help with some things. Even an older child can help around the house. If your baby's dad is home, that might be all the help you need.

You may need help with:

- Shopping for groceries and baby supplies
- Doing laundry
- Cooking
- Cleaning up
- Watching your baby while you take a shower or nap

Some people aren't very helpful. They make life harder for you. Sometimes they make more work for you. Or they upset you by not understanding what you're going through. Try to keep people away who aren't helpful. This is no time to entertain or get more stressed. If you don't have enough help, ask your caregivers or the hospital staff about where to call for help at home.

Advice to Helpers (Family and Friends)

Your support and love are important to the new mother. Here are a few helpful hints:

- A new mother needs to hear that she's doing a good job. When she does something "right," tell her.
- Offer help, especially if she can't (or won't) ask for it.
- Ask her how you can help (preparing meals, doing laundry, shopping, or cleaning).
- Don't spend all your time holding and caring for the baby, unless she can't. Instead, help her learn to take care of her new baby.
- Let her take care of the baby in her own way. She may choose to do things differently than you.
- Plan to work hard, sleep little, and leave tired! She'll appreciate all you've done.

Staying Healthy after the Birth

What can you do to feel better and recover quickly after having a baby?

Get Enough Rest and Sleep

Getting enough sleep is a big problem for new mothers and fathers. Lack of sleep slows your physical and emotional recovery. Try to sleep whenever you can. If you can't sleep, at least lie down and rest. Rest can give you the energy you need to take care of yourself and your baby.

All babies need to wake up and feed at night. Some babies seem to sleep more during the day than at night. Try not to worry. Gradually your baby will need to feed less at night and will sleep longer. Your job is to get as much sleep as you can even though you have to wake up to feed your baby.

A Reminder

Rest and sleep give you the energy you need and make early parenthood easier.

Here are some helpful hints on how to get enough sleep:

- Think about how much sleep you usually need each day (6 hours? 8 hours?). That's the amount of sleep you should try to get after your baby's born. It won't be all at one time, but it can add up over the course of the night and into the day.

- Plan to stay in bed (or keep going back to bed) until you've slept enough. This means not getting up except for caring for your baby, eating meals, and making trips to the bathroom. You may have to stay in bed from 10 P.M. until noon the next day to get the amount of sleep you need!

- If you're worried about not hearing your baby's cries, try keeping your baby close to you while you sleep. In the first weeks, babies usually sleep more when they're with their parents.

- Try to sleep or rest when your baby sleeps—even during the daytime. This may seem hard if you're used to sleeping only at night. Plan on lying down during the day if you don't get enough sleep at night.

- Rest or sleep before doing other things. Someone else can do the laundry and dishes. Or let these things wait until you've had a nap.

- Let others hold and care for your baby while you rest.

- If you have other children, your best chance for sleep is to have someone watch them while you nap.

✹ Tanya's Story ✹

I was worried about having a 3-year-old and a new baby. It seemed that Molly needed so much from me. I didn't know how I could take care of a little baby, too. Jason got only 2 weeks off from work. We were both tired and busy, but we managed. We're a pretty good team. Our friends brought us food, which was great.

Molly didn't pay much attention to the baby. Sometimes she ignored me, too. I know she didn't mean it, but it hurt my feelings. She liked playing with her dad. It was tough for Molly when Jason went back to work. Even if I couldn't play as much, I could talk and listen to her while taking care of the baby. It was nice when a friend invited Molly over to her house. Molly liked playing with her kids, and I got a break.

Sit-Back Exercise

A week or two after the birth, begin doing this exercise. It helps your tummy muscles get stronger.

1. Sit with your knees bent and your feet flat on the floor.

2. Hold your baby close to your chest, or rest her on your legs. (If you do this exercise without your baby, stretch your arms out in front of you.)

3. Slowly lean back about halfway to the floor. (Or stop when you begin to feel unsteady or your tummy muscles feel weak.)

4. Stay leaning back for a slow count of 5.

5. Sit back up.

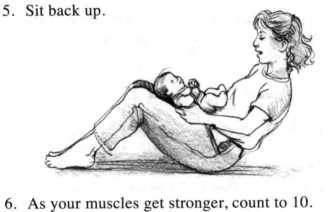

6. As your muscles get stronger, count to 10. Then work toward doing 5 sit-backs during each exercise session.

Exercise to Help Get Back in Shape

If your labor and birth were normal, it's safe to begin doing mild exercises within a day or so. You don't have to, though. It's all right to wait a few weeks. Start gradually and do what makes you feel good. Do your Kegels. Take a walk. Do some exercises that strengthen your tummy muscles.

You know you're overdoing it if the exercises make you very tired, cause pain, or increase your vaginal bleeding. If that happens, take it easy for a few days and start exercising again, but not so hard. Of course, if any of these problems remain after taking it easy, call your caregiver.

If you had a cesarean birth, you'll need to wait longer before you begin exercising. Follow your caregiver's advice about exercise and other activities such as driving, stair climbing, and lifting.

Eat Healthy Foods

Continue to eat well after your baby is born (as described on pages 36–40). Follow your caregiver's advice about taking your prenatal vitamins and iron pills.

To lose extra pounds after the birth, you don't have to go on a strict diet. Most new mothers lose weight gradually over several months as long as they don't eat a lot more than they need. If you want to lose weight, losing 1–2 pounds per week is a good plan.

If you're breastfeeding, eat good foods so you stay healthy. You'll make healthy breast milk even if your diet isn't perfect. But if you eat poorly, nutrients will be taken from your body's supply to make milk. After a while, this will affect your health. So, to keep feeling good when you're breastfeeding, try these suggestions:

1. Eat a variety of healthy foods.

2. Eat enough to maintain your weight. (You may need to eat more than you usually do.)

3. Eat what tastes good.

4. Drink plenty of water and other fluids. If you feel thirsty, drink something. You know you're getting enough if your pee is light yellow. If you're not getting enough, your pee will be dark yellow.

You may wonder if certain foods should be avoided or could cause problems for your breastfed baby. You may be told to avoid eating cabbage, broccoli, and spicy foods because they cause more gas and make your baby fussy. That's usually not true. In fact, many mothers will tell you that their babies do well when they eat spicy foods or cabbage! Usually the foods you eat are fine for breastfeeding.

What should you NOT have when you're breastfeeding? Alcohol, the chemicals in cigarettes (such as nicotine), and other drugs go into breast milk and harm new babies. It's best to limit or avoid using them in the early months of breastfeeding. Caffeine affects sleep, but usually a small amount doesn't have much effect on your baby. If you want coffee, tea, or a cola, try drinking 1–2 cups a day and see if it makes any difference in your baby's sleep pattern.

Some babies are fussy if their mothers eat large amounts of certain foods. Be careful about eating large amounts, such as a half flat of strawberries, a quart of juice, or a lot of chocolate. Try to eat normal-size servings of many different foods.

If you think a certain food is bothering your baby, stop eating it. Wait a few days and see if your baby seems better. If it doesn't make any difference, try that food again and see how your baby reacts. Also, talk to your caregiver or a breastfeeding counselor if you have questions about what to eat.

Pay Attention to Your Feelings and Emotions

After the birth, you may be surprised at how moody you are. You may be excited, tired, and irritated—all at the same time. You may cry over little things. These ups and downs are caused by changes in your hormones—and the big life changes that come with having a baby. For most women, these feelings are mild and go away within a week or so. For others, they last longer and sometimes get worse.

Baby Blues

Baby blues are common. About 8 out of 10 new mothers have them. The blues often occur in the first week after birth. When you have baby blues:

- You cry easily.
- You feel like you can't do everything.
- You wonder if you are a good mother.

Baby blues are normal, and they're usually over within 2 weeks after birth. Here are some suggestions to help you feel better when you have the baby blues:

- Get as much sleep or rest as you can.
- Reduce any pain that you're feeling:
  - * For more on vaginal pain, see pages 168–169.
  - * For more on breast pain, see page 170.
  - * For more on pain after a cesarean, see pages 161–163.
- Ask family and friends to help with the housework and baby care.

❧ Cami's Story ❧

The hardest thing for me was being alone all day with Tommy. Jeff had to go right back to work. I got so tired. Sometimes when Tommy cried, I cried, too. I had wanted a baby, but sometimes I wished I hadn't had him. I felt like a terrible mother. When I got more sleep, I felt better. Then I wondered how I could have felt unhappy about being a mother.

Postpartum Mood Disorders

Postpartum mood disorder (*PPMD*) is a term used for emotional problems that occur after birth and are serious enough for a woman to need professional help. *Postpartum depression* is the best-known form of PPMD. About 2 in 10 women have a postpartum mood disorder. So, it's not as common as having the blues.

Often a postpartum mood disorder begins between 6 weeks and 6 months after the birth. However, it can start anytime between a few weeks and 1 year after the birth. You or a family member might be the first one to notice the signs that something isn't right.

Signs of a Postpartum Mood Disorder

- Feeling very upset and worried
- Having no energy
- Not feeling hungry, forgetting to eat meals, or eating a lot
- Having trouble sleeping, even when you're very tired
- Crying a lot more than usual
- Yelling or being angry at family or friends
- Not being interested in anything, even caring for your baby
- Having panic attacks (difficulty breathing, trouble swallowing, racing heartbeat)
- Having thoughts of hurting yourself or your baby
- Having flashbacks about difficult times in the past or during the birth

There are good ways to treat PPMD, especially if treatment starts early. Treatment ranges from things you can do for yourself to counseling and/or medication.

What to Do If You Have a Postpartum Mood Disorder

1. Realize that you're not a bad mother. It's not your fault that you're having some of the thoughts or feelings described in the last section.

2. Be good to yourself by:

   - Eating well (avoiding alcohol and caffeine)
   - Getting plenty of rest and sleep
   - Going outside into natural light
   - Getting regular exercise (taking a walk for 20 minutes or more)
   - Having time for yourself (getting away from chores and baby care for a while)
   - Being with loving family and friends

3. Tell a trusted person how you're feeling, especially if you're worried about hurting yourself or your baby.

4. Ask your caregiver or a social worker about therapists and support groups that can help you.

5. If needed, see a doctor or mental health specialist about counseling or taking medicine.

Finding a New Mother's Support Group

Support groups help women realize they're not alone. You or a friend can reach the national organization Postpartum Support International by visiting their website at www.postpartum.net. Also, your local hospital, health department, or caregiver can tell you about support groups in your area.

Family Planning and Sex after the Birth

Some women want to have sex soon after the birth. However, most women prefer to wait a while. They're afraid that it'll hurt, or they're too tired. Doctors and midwives tell you to wait until your stitches are healed and your vaginal flow (lochia) is almost gone. This takes about 4–6 weeks. Of course, you should wait until you feel like having sex. The problem is that many new mothers aren't interested in sex, but their partners may be. Try to be honest and kind to each other when you talk about it.

In the beginning, a sore vagina and tiredness affect your desire for sex and your pleasure in making love. Don't worry that you've lost your desire for sex—it will come back. If your vagina hurts during sex, try being on top of your partner. This puts less pressure on the back of your vagina (where stitches are done for a tear or episiotomy).

Also, it's normal for your vagina to be dry after birth when you're breastfeeding. This happens because you normally have less estrogen during breastfeeding and this decreases your vaginal *secretions* (fluids and mucus). Vaginal dryness may cause pain during intercourse. You can put a water-soluble lubricant like K-Y Jelly or Astroglide into your vagina or on your partner's penis. This helps take away the pain caused by dryness. You can buy vaginal jelly or cream at a drugstore. But don't use ones with estrogen; they might reduce your milk supply.

To give your body a chance to recover from being pregnant, try to wait at least 1 year before getting pregnant again. Remember that you can get pregnant before your menstrual periods return. Birth control pills or patches containing estrogen prevent pregnancy, but they can affect your breast milk supply. So, don't use them when breastfeeding. However, if you need to use emergency contraception (taking birth control medicine after unprotected sex), talk to your caregiver about how it affects breastfeeding.

Let your caregiver know if you're breastfeeding. He or she can help you choose a safe and easy family planning method. These methods of birth control are safe to use during breastfeeding:

- Mini-pill (low-dose birth control pill)
- Depo-Provera shots
- Condom along with *spermicidal* (sperm-killing) foam, cream, or jelly
- Diaphragm
- Cervical cap
- IUD (a small plastic device put into your uterus during a vaginal exam)

Having a Baby Changes Your Life

Being a new parent brings a mixture of feelings—excitement, exhaustion, fear, and joy. There's nothing like it. You feel like your life has changed overnight. Sometimes you may wish that your life would be like it used to be. It seemed so easy then!

A Special Note

Once you have a baby, your life will never be the same. But there may be some wonderful new changes. Your life will be different and it'll take a while to get used to it.

When Will I Get Back to "Normal"?

It takes time to recover physically and adjust emotionally after you have a baby. The amount of time depends on:

- Your physical and mental health
- The amount of love and help you get from family and friends
- Your experience and confidence with baby care
- Your baby's health and personality
- Your financial situation and need to return to work

If things are going well, you'll recover more quickly and adjust faster than if you're having troubles or problems. It usually takes 1–3 months to find a new balance in your life.

Parenting

Parenthood begins when you become pregnant and
lasts a lifetime. Parenting is challenging and tiring. Yet,
it's one of the most important and rewarding jobs you'll
ever have. The early weeks aren't easy. However,
a good start helps you build a strong family.
With outside help and support, you'll have
more time and energy to give to your baby.
(See pages 254–255 for information about
service agencies that can help make
parenting easier for you.)

Even if you don't know much about babies, you can learn how to be a good parent. Watch your baby. Pay attention to his behavior to find out what he wants and needs. (For more about babies, see Chapter 10.)

You can also take parenting classes. Community colleges often have them in their parent education departments. Contact your local health department or childbirth education agency to learn about parent support groups in your area.

A Note to Fathers and Partners

This early time with your new baby will be important for both of you. Spend some time learning about your baby. You'll offer your own style of parenting. The baby will know your voice and will respond to you in a special way. (See pages 249–250 for more about the father's role.) Caring for your new baby during these early months will give you lifelong memories. You'll be glad you shared in the work and joy of parenting.

CHAPTER 9

Feeding Your Baby

Milk is your baby's first food. During the first several months, your baby will have only breast milk, formula, or both. When your baby is 4–6 months old, her healthcare provider will talk to you about starting *solid foods* (baby foods). This chapter gives you helpful hints about breastfeeding and formula feeding your new baby.

Breastfeeding

Breastfeeding is the best way to feed your baby. Any amount of breast milk is better than none. So, if you're interested in breastfeeding, try it right after your baby is born. It's easier to start and stop breastfeeding than it is to never breastfeed and wish that you had.

Why is breast milk so good?

- Breast milk is the perfect food for babies. It's made for human babies.
- Breast milk is always available. And after a few weeks, it's easier than mixing formula to make a bottle.
- Breast milk is clean and safe for your baby.
- Breast milk helps your baby fight germs and sickness.
- Breast milk helps prevent allergies.

Breastfeeding is also good for you. It helps reduce your risk of getting certain diseases such as breast cancer or cancer of your *ovaries* (sex glands inside your belly). Breastfeeding also costs less than formula. So you save money. In addition, breastfeeding creates a special bond between you and your baby. You'll both enjoy the closeness.

Making Breast Milk

Your breasts change during pregnancy to get ready for breastfeeding. By the middle months of pregnancy, you begin making *colostrum* (your baby's first milk in the days right after birth). Colostrum is full of *antibodies* (germ fighters that pass from your blood to your breast milk and then to your baby). Colostrum also has nutrients such as vitamins, protein, and healthy fat. Colostrum is thick and rich. So your baby needs only a little bit of it.

After a few days, the yellowish colostrum becomes whiter and you begin making a lot more milk. It's just the right mixture of nutrients for your growing baby. Your breasts make as much milk as your baby needs. In fact, if you had twins, you could make enough milk for 2 babies.

The process of making breast milk is called *lactation*. A more common word for breastfeeding is *nursing* your baby. Although your breasts grow larger at first, they don't stay that way the entire time you're breastfeeding. They gradually get smaller when your baby starts taking other foods at around 6 months. When you stop breastfeeding, your breasts usually go back to their normal sizes.

> ### ✿ Tanya's Story ✿
>
> Breastfeeding was so different this time. The first time, my nipples were sore for 2 weeks and it was a real struggle. This time, I couldn't believe how fast my milk came in. The soreness was nothing like last time. But I wasn't prepared for the afterpains! Every time I fed my baby, I had bad cramps in my belly. After several days, the cramps stopped. What a relief! Then breastfeeding was easy.

Getting Started

The first feeding is special. It's usually the first thing
you do for your new baby. After the first couple of hours
following birth, your baby probably won't be as interested
in eating as he was at first. By the second day, most
babies wake up and become eager to nurse again.

Here are some ways to make the first feedings easier:

- Breastfeed your baby right after birth.
  Babies are alert and awake in the first hour.

- Get into a comfortable position. Use pillows
  to support your arms and your baby.

- Have your nurse or midwife help you with the
  first feeding if breastfeeding is new to you.

- Have visitors leave during the feeding if you
  want to be alone as you learn to breastfeed.

Most babies know how to nurse right from the start.
Some seem sleepy or have trouble latching on to the
breast. If you need help, ask your nurse or a breastfeeding
specialist to help you. With time and practice, you'll get
better at it and so will your baby.

The early feedings may be different from what you expected. Your baby may only lick your breast. Or he might latch on, tug, and suck vigorously. You may be surprised at how strongly your baby suckles your nipple.

Holding Your Baby While Nursing

There are several positions you can use while breastfeeding your baby. You may want to ask your caregiver or nurse to show you how to do them. One position may be easier for you in the beginning, but you'll probably use most of them at one time or another.

Cradle hold. Your baby's head rests in the crook of your arm. Your arm supports his back and your hand keeps his bottom close to your belly.

Alternate cradle hold. Your baby's head rests in your hand with your fingers and thumb near his neck. Your arm supports your baby's back and your elbow keeps his bottom near your belly.

Alternate cradle hold

Football hold. With your baby at your side, hold his head in your hand and support his back with your arm. Have your baby rest his bottom on a pillow or your hip.

Lying on your side. Your baby rests on the bed next to you. His mouth is close to your breast and his body is near your chest and belly.

Football hold

Helping Your Baby Get a Good Latch

Latch is the way your baby's mouth holds on to your breast as she nurses. If it's a good latch, your baby gets milk and it doesn't hurt your nipples. Some babies get onto the nipple and *areola* (the dark area around the nipple) without much trouble. Others need help to get a good latch.

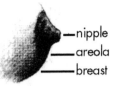
—nipple
—areola
——breast

Here are some suggestions for getting your baby onto your breast with a good latch:

1. Bring your baby to your breast. Hold her so she's facing your breast without turning her head. If you are holding her in a cradle hold, think "belly to belly". This helps keep her head in the right position.

2. Hold your baby close with your hand under her head (near her neck) and your arm against her back. (This is the alternate cradle hold.)

3. With your other hand, hold your breast. Make this hand into a C shape and put your thumb on your breast at the edge of the areola. Then put your fingers at the edge of the areola on the other side of your breast. Don't touch your areola. Next, gently squeeze your fingers and thumb together making a "breast sandwich."

4. Stroke your baby's lips with your nipple to get her to open her mouth wide.

5. When her mouth is open WIDE, put your areola onto her lower lip. Then quickly roll her onto your breast. Make sure she has both the nipple and a lot of the areola in her mouth.

6. With a good latch, her lower jaw and chin press against your breast and her nose almost touches it. (See the pictures on page 196.)

7. Let your baby suckle for as long as she likes. (10–20 minutes is common.) She may come off your breast on her own. If she still wants to eat, offer your other breast. She may nurse from 1 breast or both.

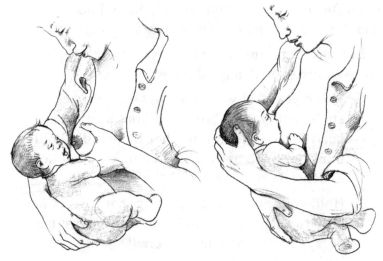

Getting a good latch using the cradle hold

If your baby doesn't get a large part of the areola in her mouth, your nipple will probably hurt. So, take her off and try again. To take your baby off your breast, slip your finger into her mouth to break the suction. Then pull her away from your breast. Before long, you and your baby will get a good latch every time. Remember, you need to have a good latch to keep your nipples from getting sore and cracked. (See pages 209–210 for more about sore nipples and ways to prevent and treat them.)

How to Know When to Feed Your Baby

Feed your baby whenever he wants to eat. He'll use *hunger cues* (physical signs) to tell you when he wants milk. For example, he'll show you he's hungry by sucking on anything close to his mouth. Or he'll make little sounds and try to suck on his hands. Or he'll suck on his blanket or your arm. If you miss these early hunger cues, he'll begin to fuss and then finally cry. Try to feed your baby before he cries. It's harder to feed him when he's crying.

How often will your baby eat? Here are some guidelines about feeding patterns in the early weeks:

- Most new babies nurse every 1–3 hours. However, babies don't always eat on a regular schedule. Sometimes a baby will eat every hour for several feedings and then sleep for 3–4 hours.

- Most newborns nurse between 8 and 18 times a day. It's common to have about 12 feedings each day. After several weeks, your baby will be able to take in more milk at each feeding. This usually reduces the number of feedings each day.

- Let your baby nurse at each breast for as long as he wants. Longer feedings help your baby get plenty of milk. Feedings may last 20–40 minutes or longer.

- The length of a feeding often depends on your baby's size and feeding style. Some babies suck hard and fast and have shorter feedings. Others suck a little, pause, and suck again. Other babies fall asleep at the breast and then wake up and nurse again. It takes these babies a long time to get enough milk.

It's easier to feed your baby when he wants to eat rather than feeding him on a schedule. Trying to make a hungry baby wait until a certain time to nurse will be upsetting for both of you. Also, it's hard to wake a baby for a feeding. You don't need to wake your baby unless he's losing weight or has jaundice. If your baby has jaundice, he may sleep through a feeding time. So, in the first weeks, awaken your baby if he sleeps over 4 hours.

Babies have *growth spurts* that last 2–7 days. During these times, your baby is growing faster and needs to eat more often. Growth spurts occur at about 3 weeks, 6 weeks, 3 months, and 6 months of age. At these times, your baby may nurse every hour or so. His frequent feedings tell your breasts to make more milk. This increases your milk supply, and your baby gets more milk at each feeding. When you're making enough milk, he'll go back to having fewer feedings.

These growth spurts may make you feel like you're feeding all the time. However, as your baby grows and takes more milk at each feeding, you'll begin to feel that you have more time for yourself between feedings.

Breastfeeding Basics

Begin each feeding on the breast you ended with at the last feeding (or the breast that feels most full). Sometimes babies will nurse from only 1 breast at each feeding. If your baby nurses from both breasts, she usually takes more milk from the first one. By switching back and forth between breasts when you start a feeding, you make sure both breasts are making plenty of milk.

Nurse from the first breast for as long as your baby wants to suckle (usually about 10–20 minutes). When the milk flow slows down, you may notice she's swallowing less. Also, your breast feels softer when you press on it. Let your baby slide off your breast on her own.

After she stops feeding on 1 breast, burp her to help get air out of her tummy. You may also want to change her diaper at this time. If she fell asleep after the first breast, a diaper change may wake her for more feeding. Then offer the other breast. Let her nurse as long as she's awake and interested. If she doesn't take the second breast, don't worry. She doesn't need the extra milk. During growth spurts, babies often feed from both breasts during each feeding.

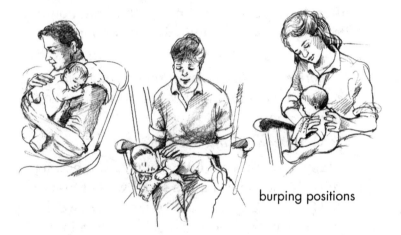

burping positions

Is Your Baby Getting Enough Milk?

Generally, mothers make enough milk for their babies. It may take a day or two of extra feedings to increase your milk supply during a growth spurt. But that extra nursing is the key to increasing your milk supply. Frequent breastfeeding makes more milk. Giving your baby formula will prevent your milk supply from catching up with your baby's needs.

During the first week or so after the birth, you'll want to make sure that you're making enough milk. Watch for these signs that help you know if your baby is getting enough milk:

- *He feeds at least 8 times each day.* Most babies feed more often (8–18 times in 24 hours).

- *He has at least 6 wet diapers each day* (after 5 days of age). If you're using disposable diapers, it's hard to tell how often your baby is peeing. Put a small piece of paper towel in the diaper. It stays wet if your baby has peed.

- *He has at least 2 poopy diapers each day.* Many babies have frequent bowel movements, often 1 after every feeding. In the first month, it's common to see yellowish, soft poop after almost every feeding.

- *He actively sucks and swallows throughout the feeding.* Listen for swallowing. It sounds like an *ugh* sound.

- *He seems content after feedings.*

Your baby's weight gain tells you that he's getting enough milk. Most babies have a small weight loss right after birth. They usually are back to their birth weight by 2 weeks. Your baby's caregiver should see him in the first week or two after birth. At that visit, the doctor will weigh and measure your baby and make sure he's healthy. You may also return for a visit at the hospital, have a home visit, or receive a visit from a public health nurse. You may want to go to your WIC clinic to check your baby's weight.

✷ Jenny's Story ✷

I decided to try breastfeeding. I heard it was easier and really good for babies. But it wasn't easy at first! I couldn't tell if I was doing it right. I was worried that Emily wasn't getting enough milk. I thought I was starving her! My mom didn't breastfeed me, so she couldn't help me much at first. I kept calling the clinic with questions. When Emily was about a week old, they told me to come in and see a nurse who helps women with breastfeeding problems. She really helped me. I found out I wasn't doing such a bad job after all.

Emily had lost a little weight. But the nurse said it's normal for babies to lose some weight in the first few days. She said my breasts had lots of milk, so I could stop worrying. Mom listened to all the advice so she could help me more. After that, I took Emily in for a couple of weight checks. She kept gaining weight, and breastfeeding got easier after a couple of weeks. I'm glad I breastfed Emily. Kyle's proud of me, too.

How to Know If Your Baby Is NOT Getting Enough Milk

- She feeds fewer than 8 times in 24 hours.

- She has dark yellow urine. And she doesn't have at least 1 wet diaper for each day old she is (for the first week or so). For example, expect to see at least 3 wet diapers when your baby is 3 days old.

- She hasn't had a bowel movement in a 24-hour period in the first few days after birth.

- She's sleepy and not interested in feeding.

- Her face, chest, and the whites of her eyes are yellowish. (Having yellow eyes is a clear sign of jaundice. *Jaundice* occurs when there is too much bilirubin in your baby's blood. This can happen when she doesn't get enough to eat and she doesn't get rid of the blackish green poop that was in her bowels before she was born.)

Reminders

Call your baby's doctor right away if you think your baby isn't getting enough milk or is yellow. In the first week after birth, doctors watch babies for 2 problems that are caused by not getting enough milk. One problem is jaundice, and the other is *dehydration* (becoming dried out). You can make sure your baby gets the help she needs by reporting your concerns.

Don't give your baby a bottle of water. Breast milk contains all the water your baby needs. Water can make your baby feel full so she doesn't want to nurse. This can lead to poor weight gain and jaundice.

If you're worried about your baby's weight because she isn't feeding well and isn't having lots of wet and poopy diapers, call your caregiver and share your concerns. He or she may ask you to bring your baby into the office or clinic to weigh and examine her. Expect to see about 1 ounce of weight gain per day since your baby was checked the last time. If your baby isn't gaining weight well, ask about getting help from a breastfeeding expert.

Getting Help with Breastfeeding

Most new mothers need help with breastfeeding. There are plenty of breastfeeding specialists and support groups to help you and your baby:

- Most cities have *lactation consultants* who are trained to care for breastfeeding mothers and babies. Most lactation consultants have passed an exam and have a certificate as an International Board Certified Lactation Consultant (IBCLC). For more information or to find a lactation consultant in your area, contact the International Lactation Consultant Association (ILCA). (See page 254.)

- Ask your childbirth educator to help you find a breastfeeding expert. Ask for someone who is an IBCLC or who has experience helping breastfeeding women.

- Talk to your midwife, doctor, or nurse at the hospital. They may offer breastfeeding advice or help you find a breastfeeding specialist.

- Contact your local WIC office or National Healthy Mothers, Healthy Babies Coalition agency. (See page 254 for more information.)

- Call your local La Leche League (LLL) group. They offer breastfeeding tips and can tell you which LLL leaders are IBCLC qualified. (See page 254 for more information.)

- Family members and friends can also provide support and encouragement with breastfeeding.

Breastfeeding Tips

Almost every woman has questions and concerns about breastfeeding in the first weeks and months. The following hints may help you solve some of your breastfeeding problems.

Decreasing Breast Fullness/Engorgement

When your colostrum changes to milk, your breasts become heavy, full, and tender. This happens between 2 and 4 days after birth. It's normal to have some discomfort and swelling at this time. But if your breasts become hard and painful, this isn't normal. This is called *engorgement*.

Try to nurse often (even before your milk comes in) to help prevent engorgement. When your breasts get very full, your nipples become swollen and don't stick out. This condition (sometimes called *flat nipples*) can make it harder for your baby to latch on to your breasts. Or your baby may not be able to nurse at all.

What can you do?

- The best way to relieve breast fullness and tenderness is to nurse frequently.
- Soften your nipple and areola by *hand expressing* (squeezing out) a few drops of milk. Put your fingers and thumb on the edges of your areola and squeeze firmly, but not too hard. This presses some drops of milk out of your breast and softens the areola, making it easier for your baby to latch on.

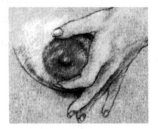

- Take a warm shower to help your milk begin dripping from your breasts. This helps make the areolas softer so your baby can latch on.

- Once your baby is nursing, use gentle pressure on your breasts to encourage milk flow. (See Encouraging Milk Flow below for a description of how to do this.)

- Let your baby nurse as long as he wants on the first breast. When he stops swallowing or falls asleep, take him off and put him on the other side. If he doesn't nurse from the other breast, hand express or use a breast pump to get some milk out of that breast.

- After nursing, apply a cool cloth or ice pack to your breasts to reduce tenderness and swelling. Some doctors and midwives suggest taking ibuprofen (a pain pill that also helps reduce the swelling).

The swollen, tender feeling usually lasts about a day or 2. If your baby can't nurse even after you've pumped your breasts, get help. A lactation consultant or another person who knows about breastfeeding should be able to help you relieve the engorgement.

Encouraging Milk Flow

Most of the time, your breasts will work just fine without extra help. But if you want to get more milk out, try putting pressure on your breast during a feeding to help milk flow toward your nipple. This is sometimes called breast massage. However, don't rub in circles like you do with most massages. Instead, press gently from the outer area of your breast toward your nipple. Stop before you get to the areola. Pressing too close to the areola can change your baby's latch.

Pressure behind the milk-producing glands (located at the outer edges of your breasts) helps with several breastfeeding problems:

- It relieves breast fullness.
- It gives your baby more milk and increases your milk supply.
- It encourages a sleepy baby to continue nursing.
- It reduces the discomfort of a plugged duct or *mastitis* (infected breast).

There are a couple ways of using pressure on your breasts:

- Breast pressure: Put the palm of your hand on your ribs near the outer edge of your breast. Then slide it a little onto your breast. Press on your breast with your hand. When your baby begins to suckle less, move your hand to another part of your breast and press again.

- Breast compression: Make your hand into a C shape and cup your breast. With your palm on your ribs, put your fingers and thumb near the outer edge of your breast. Squeeze your fingers and thumb together. When your baby begins to suckle less, move your hand and compress again.

Here's how to encourage milk flow during a feeding:

1. Once your baby has latched on and is sucking, you'll notice that she stops sometimes. Pay attention to these pauses in her sucking.

2. When she pauses, gently press against the milk glands in the upper part of your breast near your arm. This will make more milk come down. You'll also notice a burst of sucking as milk is pressed toward the nipple and into your baby's mouth.

3. When your baby pauses again, press again. If needed, move your hand to another section and use pressure or compression in that area.

✿ Jenny's Story ✿

I was worried that my baby wasn't getting enough milk, so the nurse at the clinic helped me put Emily on my breast. Not only did Emily get more milk, the pain in my nipples went away. The nurse told me to wait and wait and wait some more until Emily opened her mouth really wide. The nurse also helped me squeeze the areola before Emily latched on to my breast. This helped Emily get more of the areola in her mouth. Boy, it sure was great to have someone help me.

Increasing Your Milk Supply

As your baby grows and gains weight, he'll need more milk. You'll probably make plenty of milk, but your baby may be fussy for a few days while you build up your supply. How do you increase your breast milk supply? You make more milk when your baby takes more milk from your breasts. This is called "supply and demand." Your milk supply naturally increases in response to your baby's demand and need for more milk.

If you feel you need to increase your supply, try the following suggestions:

- Breastfeed more often than you have been. Giving more milk to your baby tells your breasts to make more milk.

- Make each feeding longer. Let your baby feed for as long as he wants. If needed, switch from 1 side to the other and then back again.

- Check your baby's latch. You should be able to hear him swallowing as he feeds. If you don't hear swallowing, try again until he's latched well and you hear him swallowing. (More swallowing means he's getting more milk.)

- Take your baby to bed with you. This gives you time to rest and a chance to pay close attention to his feeding cues. Also, having your baby's skin touching your skin helps increase your milk supply. Have him wear only a diaper, and don't have any clothing over your breasts. A blanket will keep both of you warm.

- Press on your breast while feeding (as described on page 206). This increases the amount of milk for your baby at each feeding.

- Pump your breasts after feedings, especially if your baby won't stay on your breast when your supply is low. Pump about 10–15 minutes per side using a good breast pump. If your baby is unable to breastfeed, pump some breast milk and give it to him in a bottle.

- Don't give your baby formula. This will cause your breasts to make less milk.

- Get help from a lactation consultant or breastfeeding expert to help build up your milk supply.

Avoiding Sore Nipples

Most new mothers have some nipple soreness during the first week or so. When your baby sucks on the nipple, you may feel a burning pain at the beginning of a feeding. The stretching of the nipple and areola causes this pain. It usually goes away when the milk begins to flow. This nipple soreness should stop after several weeks.

To help reduce the pain, hand express a few drops of milk to soften the areola before feeding. Try to do this before every feeding during the first week after the birth. In addition, follow the suggestions on pages 195–196 to help your baby latch on well. In the first weeks of breastfeeding, a poor latch is the most common cause of pain that lasts for the entire feeding.

Here are some ways to prevent and treat sore nipples:

- Correct the latch. Shape the nipple and areola so your baby gets your nipple and a large part of your areola in his mouth. Be sure his mouth is open wide when he latches on. (See pages 195–196.) If a poor latch is the problem, the pain will go away as soon as you fix the latch.

- Feed your baby often. If you wait until your breasts are very full, it will be harder for your baby to latch on.

- Begin feeding on the less-sore side. A baby's suck is usually stronger at the beginning of each feeding.

- Express some milk before feeding to soften the areola and make latching on easier.

- When taking your baby off your breast, slip your finger into his mouth to break the suction. This will help you get your nipple out of his mouth without pain.

If you have other problems (such as flat nipples, bleeding nipples, or sucking difficulties), contact a lactation consultant or breastfeeding expert. You may need to be seen by someone who can help you with the latch. Also, a consultant can suggest ways to help heal cracked or bleeding nipples.

Breastfeeding in Public

At first, you may have trouble breastfeeding without taking off your shirt and bra. After a few weeks, breastfeeding will be easier and you'll be able to keep your clothes on. Then you'll be able to breastfeed your baby when visitors come or when you go out.

If you're concerned about breastfeeding in front of others, here are some ways to help you feel more comfortable:

- Wear a nursing bra that unhooks above the breast. This will allow you to lower the flap without taking off your bra.

- Wear a loose-fitting shirt to cover your breast while you're breastfeeding.

- Take along a small blanket or shawl to put over your shoulder and cover your baby and breast.

- Practice feeding in front of a mirror. You'll see what others see when you breastfeed. When you're sure your breast is covered, you'll be more comfortable feeding in front of others.

- Try feeding in front of a friend, another breastfeeding mom, or a family member at first. When you're comfortable feeding in front of this person, then you'll be ready to feed in public situations.

Pumping and Storage

From time to time, a mother may want a break from breastfeeding. Or she wants to collect her milk when she's at work. Most mothers use a breast pump. Others use hand expression to collect breast milk. Either way you'll have breast milk so someone else can put it in a bottle for your baby. Whichever method you use, it's best to wait until your baby is breastfeeding well, which is about 3–4 weeks after the birth.

Pumping or hand expressing becomes easier with practice. It may take a while to learn how to do it effectively. You need clean hands and clean equipment (bottles, bottle liners, or milk containers). Follow the directions on how to clean your pumping supplies.

Try pumping after a feeding. Choose a feeding when you have the most milk. Pump for 10–15 minutes per side. At first, you won't get much milk. However, after a few days of pumping at that same time, you'll get more milk.

Hand Expression

Expressing by hand doesn't cost anything. And you can do it anytime and almost anyplace. To hand express your breast milk:

- Place your thumb on the top edge of your areola, and your fingers below.

- Lift your breast with your fingers.

- Squeeze your breast between the pads of your thumb and fingers. Squeeze for 5–10 seconds. To keep your fingers from slipping to the end of your nipple, gently press your breast toward your chest.

- Keep squeezing off and on until the milk stops dripping or squirting out.

- Collect your milk in a measuring cup or another clean container.

- Repeat this process until the milk stops coming out or you have the milk you need.

- At first, you may get only a few drops. With practice, you'll get a steady spray.

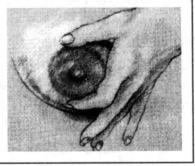

Breast milk can be stored in clean glass or plastic bottles or feeding bags that are made to store breast milk. How long can you keep your expressed breast milk?

Guidelines for storing fresh milk (milk that has just come from your breasts)

- 10 hours out of the refrigerator, if your room isn't too hot (If your room is warmer than 72°F, it can be kept out only a few hours.)
- 8 days in the refrigerator
- 3 months in a freezer that keeps ice cream hard

Label the bottle or container with the date you expressed the milk. Use fresh milk first, then the oldest frozen milk next. If frozen for a long time (over 3 months), breast milk loses some nutrients and antibodies to fight infection. Still, it's far more nutritious than formula.

To thaw frozen breast milk, place the bottle in warm water. The water should be hot but not boiling. As the water cools, add more warm water. Never thaw it in the microwave or in a pan on the stove. Overheating your milk takes away some of its special qualities and may burn your baby's mouth. Once thawed, gently swirl the milk to mix it because the fat usually floats to the top during freezing. Breast milk can be room temperature or slightly warmer when you feed it to your baby.

After thawing milk, use it right away. Or keep it for only 24 hours in the refrigerator. Don't refreeze it.

Having Support for Breastfeeding

It's very important to have the support of your partner or a family member. You're more likely to succeed at breastfeeding if the person living with you encourages your efforts to breastfeed. To increase your chances of breastfeeding for as long as you want to, find people who are enthusiastic about breastfeeding. Talk with them as much as possible in the first weeks after the birth. With help and support, learning to breastfeed is easier. And the challenges don't seem so hard to handle.

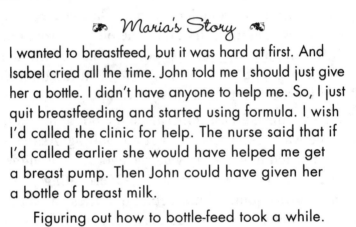

❧ Maria's Story ❧

I wanted to breastfeed, but it was hard at first. And Isabel cried all the time. John told me I should just give her a bottle. I didn't have anyone to help me. So, I just quit breastfeeding and started using formula. I wish I'd called the clinic for help. The nurse said that if I'd called earlier she would have helped me get a breast pump. Then John could have given her a bottle of breast milk.

Figuring out how to bottle-feed took a while. I always wanted Isabel to finish the whole bottle. I didn't want to waste it. But at the clinic they told me that when she stops, she's done. They were right. After that, I relaxed and then bottle-feeding was easier.

Formula Feeding

Most new mothers start out breastfeeding. When their babies are older, they sometimes give breast milk in a bottle. Some families give a bottle of formula for one or more feedings. This section is about feeding with a bottle and using formula safely.

For the first year of life, your baby should drink breast milk or iron-fortified formula. Other milk such as whole milk, 2% milk, or goat's milk is not good for babies. And it doesn't have the right mixture of vitamins, minerals, and nutrients.

Most infant formulas are made from cow's milk or soybeans. If your baby is healthy and not allergic to cow's milk, the best choice is an iron-fortified cow's milk formula. If you want your baby on a vegetarian diet with no animal protein, you might choose a soy formula with iron. (Though the words *iron-fortified* might not be on the front label.) Soy formulas are also good if a baby can't digest milk sugar. This very rare condition is called *galactosemia*.

If your baby has a milk allergy, his doctor may suggest a *hypoallergenic* formula (doesn't cause an allergic reaction). This type of formula is also iron-fortified, but it costs more than other formulas. Examples of these formulas are Nutramigen and Alimentum.

Some parents think that an iron-fortified formula causes constipation and gas. They think a low-iron formula might be better. The truth is that there's no difference in gassiness, fussiness, or constipation between babies who get an iron-fortified formula and babies who get a low-iron formula. Also, babies who are fed a low-iron formula are at risk for *anemia* (not enough iron in their blood). Anemia can cause problems with your baby's brain and body development.

Preparing Formula

Formula comes in various forms that are equally nutritious:

- *Ready-to-feed.* This costs the most, but it's the easiest. It's useful for trips or when you're very tired.

- *Liquid concentrate.* This requires careful mixing and takes more time.

- *Powdered formula.* This costs the least, but requires careful measuring and mixing. It's useful for trips if clean, warm water is handy.

When preparing formula, carefully follow the directions on the can or package. Always use the correct amount of water when mixing formula. Using too little or too much water could make your baby sick. If your water is safe for drinking, use tap water to mix the formula. If not, boil the water first. You could also use bottled water, but don't use distilled water. It doesn't have the good minerals found in water.

Using a Bottle

Most newborn babies like their breast milk or formula warm. To heat a bottle, put it in a pan or bowl of warm water. As the water cools, add more warm water. Check the temperature by dripping a little milk out of the bottle onto your wrist. It should feel warm, not hot. As your baby grows older, he may like his milk a little cooler.

Warning

Don't use a microwave to warm a bottle. It could have hot spots that could burn your baby's mouth.

Always use clean bottles and nipples. Since there are many choices, choose the bottles, bottle liners, and nipples you like best. If your baby seems to like one better than another, choose that one. It'll make feeding easier.

If your water is safe to drink, you don't need to sterilize the bottles or use special water to wash the nipples. (*Sterilizing* means boiling the bottles to get rid of germs.) Bottles may be washed by hand or in the dishwasher. Clean the nipples by hand with hot soapy water. Rinse with hot water and let them air-dry.

Tips for Formula Feeding

Formula feeding can be enjoyable for you, your baby, and your partner. To make formula feeding go well, try these simple suggestions:

- Hold your baby with her head resting in the crook of your arm (just like breastfeeding). This closeness during feedings helps you and your baby develop a special bond of love.

- Never prop a bottle and leave your baby alone for feedings. She could choke if she's left alone with a bottle.

- Hold your baby sometimes in your right arm and sometimes in your left. Your baby will look at you when she feeds. Changing sides helps her eyes and neck muscles develop normally. (Breastfed babies do this naturally.)

- Burp your baby about halfway through the feeding. Babies who gulp air while feeding may need to burp more often. As your baby grows older, she'll be able to burp on her own.

- In the first few days, feed about every 2–3 hours (or 8–12 times per day). As your baby grows older, she'll take more at each feeding and eat less often.

- Trust your baby to "tell" you how much she needs to eat. She'll probably drink more at some feedings and less at others. When she seems full or done, stop feeding. Don't try to get her to empty every bottle. If she quickly takes all the milk at each feeding, add another ounce of formula to her bottle.

- Throw out any unused formula after the feeding. Also, use a clean bottle for each feeding. Germs can grow in the formula and make your baby sick.

- Don't add cereal to her bottle of formula— even if you heard it will get her to sleep longer. Babies shouldn't eat cereal until they're at least 4–6 months old. And when a baby starts eating cereal, it's time to learn the new skill of taking food from a spoon.

- Don't give your baby extra water. Babies don't need extra water until they begin eating solid foods. Also, don't put juice or sugary drinks into a bottle. Your baby needs milk to grow and be healthy.

Feeding your baby is more than just giving food. It's a wonderful time to watch and learn about your baby. When you respond to her need for milk, she learns that she can trust you. Feeding time also offers her a chance to be close to you and show her love. Enjoy this time with your baby. It'll be over before you know it.

Chapter 10

Caring for Your Baby

Taking care of a newborn baby may seem hard at first. It's true that babies are quite helpless. They can't use words to tell you what they need, and they can't do very much for themselves. But if you think about what your baby really needs, it's easier to figure it out. Your baby needs to be fed, kept warm and clean, and cuddled and soothed when she cries.

As much as you can, try to relax and enjoy your new baby. Over time and with experience, you'll learn the best ways of caring for your baby.

Learning about Your Baby

Until you have a baby, you might think all babies are alike. But in fact, each baby is one of a kind. Your baby looks different and responds differently than other babies. Soon you'll learn how to respond to your individual baby.

How Will Your Baby Look?

At first, your newborn baby's body will seem small and his head will seem large. Some babies have a "cone head" because their heads changed shape to fit through the birth canal. Your baby's head will return to a normal shape within a few days.

Most babies have a white, creamy substance called *vernix* on their skin right after birth. The nurse wipes most of this off, but some remains for weeks in the folds of the skin. The vernix slowly goes away on its own.

Your baby's breasts and genitals may be swollen right after birth due to your pregnancy hormones.

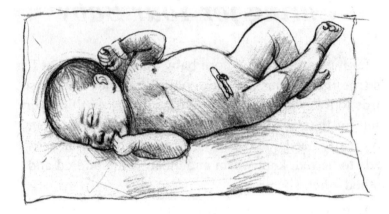

Your Baby's Abilities

For years, we thought babies couldn't do much. We believed they weren't able to tell us anything. We were wrong. Newborn babies are amazing.

Your new baby:

- *Can see you clearly if you're close to her.* She loves to look at your face. Babies are sensitive to bright lights. They usually open their eyes better when lights are turned down.

- *Can hear and respond to sounds.* She may know your voice. And she'll pay more attention to high-pitched voices. She may calm down when she hears sounds that remind her of being inside the womb (like the sounds of a dishwasher, vacuum cleaner, or when you make a loud *shhhh* sound). Your baby will also be comforted when she hears the familiar sound of a heartbeat.

- *Has a very good sense of smell and taste.* She knows your smell. The smell of your milk makes her want to suckle. Babies like the slightly sweet taste of breast milk.

- *Loves to be touched.* She enjoys being held, stroked, and cuddled. She likes to be warm, but not too hot. Most new babies like to be wrapped tightly in a blanket. This is called *swaddling.*

- *Likes movement.* It reminds her of being inside you. She enjoys being rocked, swayed, or gently bounced.

✖ Jenny's Story ✖

Right after she was born, Emily would stare at me for the longest time. At first, it seemed weird and I wondered what she was staring at. I started asking her, "What are you staring at?" She seemed to really like that. So, I started talking to her about everything, like how cute she was or what I was doing. I took her to the store when she was only 10 days old. Once, a woman started making noises to her and jiggling her feet. Emily stared at the woman for a long time. Then I said something and Emily turned to look at me. She knows me and likes my voice the best.

Your baby has several normal *reflexes*. She'll cough, sneeze, yawn, and hiccup. Many reflexes are reactions to something that happens to her. She startles or jumps at a loud noise or quick movement. She grabs your finger when you place it in her hand.

At birth, your baby can let you know what she wants, likes, and doesn't like. She does this by giving you *infant cues*. As you get to know your baby better, it'll be easier to understand her cues.

Crying is an infant cue telling you she needs or wants something. But it may mean almost anything. Her fussing and crying may be saying she's hungry, tired, lonely, uncomfortable, or overstimulated. Luckily, your baby usually gives you several gentle hints before she starts crying. Try to notice her gentle way of telling you what she needs.

Here are some common infant cues and what they mean:

- Turning toward your breast (called *rooting*), sticking out her tongue, or sucking her hand tells you she's hungry.

- Drooping eyelids tell you she's tired and may need to go to sleep.

- When she opens her eyes wide and stares at you, she's trying to get your attention. She wants you to look at her. When she's awake and calm, she likes looking at your face. If you talk or sing to her, you'll see her face light up.

- When your baby makes sounds or *coos*, she's trying to talk to you. She loves it when you make the same sounds back to her.

- When she stops looking at you, even when you're trying to get her attention, she may need a break. Babies get tired quickly even when they're having a good time. If she gets fussy when you're playing with her, slow down a bit.

When she's about 5 or 6 weeks old, she'll begin smiling at you. When you smile at her, she'll respond by smiling and cooing. Babies have an amazing ability to help their parents fall in love with them.

❧ Tanya's Story ❧

Most of the time, I could tell what Michael wanted. He really let me know when he was ready to eat. He started sucking on anything in sight, like his hand or my cheek. Once he even started sucking on his dad's nose! Jason put his nose right where Michael could get his mouth on it. What did he expect? We laughed, and Jason said, "I think you'd better feed him."

Your Baby's Personality

Your baby's size and abilities will change quickly. However, his basic nature won't change very much as he grows older. Each baby has his own personality. Some babies are very active; others are calm. Some cry and fuss more than others. Also, each baby has his own sleeping and eating schedules and his own reactions to being hungry, cold, or bored. Your child will be like a puzzle. It will take time to figure him out.

Some babies are more challenging than others. These babies have intense reactions and irregular eating and sleeping patterns. They often seem more active than other newborns. With this type of baby, it may take more time and special soothing methods to make him comfortable or help him go to sleep. Also, you may need help from family and friends with this *high-needs* baby.

As you get used to your baby, you'll find the best ways to care for him. By trying different ways to comfort your baby, you'll learn what works and what doesn't work. Most families use this *trial-and-error* method to learn about parenting.

How to Comfort Your Crying Baby

Most parents get upset when their babies cry. This is a natural reaction. Your baby's crying makes you want to take care of her. Try to respond quickly to her first cries before she gets so upset that you can't calm her easily.

❧ Maria's Story ❧

Isabel cried an awful lot when we first got home. It seemed like I could never put her down. I was so tired. All I wanted to do was sleep. I'd walk with her, rock her, and try to sing to her, but it wore me out. I was at the end of my rope! Finally, someone told me to try swaddling her. I used this stretchy baby blanket to wrap her up like a little burrito. She calmed down, especially when I said, "Shhhh," over and over again. It really helped. I swaddled her a lot in those first 2 months.

All new babies have fussy times. Often these times occur in the early or late evening. Babies cry when they're hungry, overstimulated, tired, or uncomfortable. As your baby grows older, this newborn fussiness will end.

Try these suggestions to help soothe your newborn baby:

- *Feed your baby.* Babies feed often. It might seem like a short time to you since she last fed, but it might seem like a long time to her. If she's not interested in eating, try letting her suck on your finger or a pacifier. She may need to burp, so try that, too.

- *Make sure your baby isn't too warm or too cold.* Also, check to see if she needs a diaper change.

- *Swaddle or wrap your baby in a big, lightweight baby blanket.* This may help her feel more secure. It will also remind her of being held snugly inside you during pregnancy.

- *Cuddle and hold her against your chest.* She may like hearing the sound of your heartbeat. Talking or singing to her may help. Some parents make *shhhh* sounds near their baby's ear. (This reminds babies of the sounds they heard in the womb.)

- *Use motion.* For example:

  * Hold her and sway from side to side.

  * Walk around with her in a front pack or sling.

  * Hold her in your arms as you gently bounce for several minutes. Try bouncing while standing or while sitting on a bed or exercise ball.

  * Sit in a rocking chair and rock back and forth.

  * Take her outside for a stroller ride. A car ride may also help your baby fall asleep.

  * Put her in a baby swing for a while. Make sure her head is supported as she gently swings.

- *If she seems gassy or needs to burp, try holding her in a position that puts pressure on her tummy.* For example:
  * Burp her by having her belly on your shoulder.
  * Sit down and lay her on her tummy across your lap. Gently pat her back and see if she burps or passes gas.
  * Hold her on your arm with her facing away from you. Gently sway back and forth to comfort her.

Choose one soothing method and use it for a while. Try not to overstimulate her by quickly changing from one method to another. If she continues to cry, try another technique. Hopefully you'll find the one that works. With time and practice, you'll become better at comforting your baby.

If nothing seems to calm her and you're losing your temper, take a short break. If you have help at home, let someone else try to comfort her. If not, put your baby down safely in her bed or car seat for 5–10 minutes while you calm down. **Never shake or hurt your baby.** Don't treat her roughly. Call someone (a friend or relative) to help you. Tell the person you need a break.

If you think your baby cries a lot more than other babies, talk with her doctor or the nurse at the clinic. If she cries after most feedings, take her in for a checkup. You'll find out if there are other things you can do for her, such as treating an upset stomach. You may also learn of other ways to help you cope with the crying.

Some parents worry that if they give their baby too much attention, they'll spoil her. A newborn baby can't be spoiled. She can't take care of herself. She needs you to do everything for her (feeding, dressing, bathing, and comforting). Taking care of your baby's needs is not spoiling her.

When your baby cries, she needs *more* care, not less. And the sooner you pick up a crying baby, the sooner the crying stops. By responding to her cries, you're showing her that you're listening to her. And when her needs are met, over time she'll cry less.

❧ Maria's Story ❧

The mother-baby class saved my life. I found out there are other babies just like Isabel. And other mothers are stressed out, too. The group leader talked about "high-needs" babies. That's definitely Isabel. Our leader told us that these babies settle down after a while. She told us not to think that our babies don't like us or that we're terrible mothers. I needed to hear that. Our leader also said that being home alone all day with a baby is hard. Some of the mothers in the group made plans to meet at the park once a week. It was nice to have adults around who understood what I was going through. I looked forward to our classes and going to the park.

Your Baby's Daily Care

You may be surprised at how busy you are taking care of your new baby. You may get frustrated when you think about how little time you have to do anything else. It helps to remember that most new mothers feel this way. This section describes the many things you and your baby will be doing each day. (For more information about feeding your baby, see Chapter 9.)

Sleep and Activity

Your baby's sleep pattern is affected by how often he eats. A newborn baby sleeps between 12 and 20 hours each day. But he usually sleeps for only a short time and then wakes up to eat. Remember, most newborn babies nurse about 12 or more times each day. Many babies have a few longer periods of sleep (3–4 hours) every day. Then they have some frequent feedings (every 1–2 hours) and stay awake. How long your baby sleeps is not a problem if he's getting enough milk each day and growing well.

Where your baby sleeps is a personal choice. Many parents find they get more sleep if they tuck their new baby in bed with them. In your bed, your baby stays warm and hears the comforting sounds of your breathing. As he grows older and needs you less at night, you may move him to a crib or bed of his own. You'll know the right time to move him.

Warning

If you drink alcohol, use drugs, or have taken medicines that make you sleepy, your baby must **not** sleep in the same bed with you. You could roll onto your baby without knowing it. This warning is for your partner, too.

Sudden Infant Death Syndrome (SIDS)

Almost every parent worries about SIDS. Here's what we know about SIDS:

- SIDS usually occurs while the baby is asleep or in bed.

- About 1 in every 2,000 babies dies of SIDS in the United States each year.

- Most SIDS deaths occur in babies who are between 2 and 4 months of age.

- Suffocation, spitting up, or *vaccines* (shots to prevent diseases) do not cause SIDS.

- SIDS is not caused by child abuse.

Here's what you can do to reduce your baby's risk of SIDS:

- Keep your baby away from tobacco smoke and from people and clothing that smell of smoke. This is important during pregnancy and after he's born.

- **Always place your baby on his back to sleep.** Make sure that anyone caring for your baby places him on his back to sleep.

- Keep your baby warm, but not hot. Dress him in the same amount of clothing as you're wearing plus a lightweight blanket that doesn't cover his head. A blanket sleeper worn by the baby could be used to replace the lightweight blanket.

- Remove soft toys, pillows, and comforters from his sleeping area. Don't use a lambskin for sleeping.

- Breastfeed. Breastfeeding lowers the risk of SIDS.

Wherever your baby sleeps, he needs to be on a firm surface on his back. This reduces the risk of *sudden infant death syndrome (SIDS)*, which is the unexpected death of a healthy baby. Research has shown that babies who are placed facedown on soft bedding are more likely to die of SIDS than babies who are put to sleep lying on their backs. Talk to your baby's doctor or the clinic nurse to learn more about safe sleeping places for your baby.

When your baby is awake, let him spend some time in different positions. A baby who's always on his back may get a flat spot on his head. Here are some ways to give him time off his back and to help his neck and back muscles become stronger:

- Put him on his tummy on a firm surface that allows him to lift his head. If he gets fussy, place some safe toys in front of him to look at, or lie down next to him.

- Hold your baby in your arms, a sling, or a front pack.

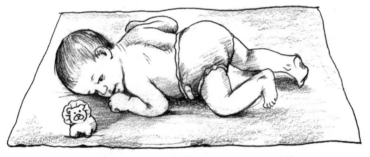

Have some tummy time when your baby is awake.

When your baby is awake, you'll be busy diapering, feeding, bathing, and dressing him. At first, your baby's schedule will seem new and different each day. After a few weeks, you'll know what to expect. Then, about the time you get used to your baby's sleep and activity patterns, they'll change again. New parenthood is never boring.

Diapering Your Baby

A baby's bowel movements are different from an
adult's. During the first day or so, your baby's poop
(called *meconium*) will be blackish green and sticky. Soon
her bowel movements will become browner. By the third
or fourth day, your baby's poop will be runnier and
yellowish. Doctors and nurses often use the term *stools*
when talking about your baby's BMs or poop.

The number and type of poopy diapers depend on the
type of milk your baby gets. Breastfed newborns usually
have runny yellow stools after most feedings (or as many
as 8–12 each day). Formula-fed newborns usually have
pasty light yellowish brown stools several times a day.
As your baby gets older, she'll poop less.

You need to change your baby's diaper every time she poops. When you change your baby's diapers, you can use cloth or disposable diapers.

1. Cloth diapers can be washed at home, or you can use a diaper service. Waterproof pants or diaper wraps are used to keep your baby's clothes dry. You can buy the wraps at the same place you buy the diapers or from the diaper service company. Diaper wraps with Velcro will keep any diaper in place. With waterproof pants that have an elastic waistband, you'll need diaper pins, clips, or fitted diapers that snap shut.

2. Disposable diapers come in a variety of sizes and styles. They have Velcro-like tabs to hold the diaper in place. Disposable diapers are easy to use, but they cost more than washing your own diapers.

Some babies get *diaper rash* when their skin becomes irritated. To prevent or treat diaper rash:

- Clean your baby's diaper area well at each diaper change. Use mild soap and water or a diaper wipe.

- Change your baby's diapers about every 2–3 hours or more often if needed.

- If you wash your own diapers, use a detergent with no perfumes and dyes (which can irritate the skin). Or rinse them twice if needed.

- If your baby is having a problem, switch to a different brand of disposable diapers to see if it's less irritating.

- Put a soothing cream or ointment on your baby's bottom when it's clean and dry. Avoid ones with *zinc oxide*. (They're usually white and very thick.) Zinc oxide is very hard to clean off and it is bad for your local water supply.

- Baby powder isn't recommended because the powder goes into the air and may hurt your baby's lungs.

Bathing Your Baby

Newborn babies need to be kept clean, but they don't need a bath every day. Babies can be given sponge baths or tub baths right from birth. Some parents find it easier to use sponge baths during the first week or so. Other parents choose a tub bath because their baby stays warmer and calmer in warm water.

✌ Jenny's Story ✌

I never thought baby care would be a problem. I used to babysit, so I thought I had it figured out. But those babies were a lot bigger than a newborn! Emily was tiny. It really helped to see how the nurse in the hospital gave her a bath. At home, Mom showed Kyle and me how to do it. We cleaned the kitchen sink and filled it several inches deep with warm water. I made sure the water wasn't too hot by feeling it with my elbow.

Mom bought a big spongy pad for the sink. That was neat. It kept Emily from sliding around. I kept my arm under her head and held her arm the whole time. I knew she'd go under if I let her go. Mom showed us how to lay a washcloth on her chest to keep her warm while she was kicking in the water. When we took her out, we learned to quickly wrap her in a baby towel to keep her warm. Emily really likes bath time.

Cord Care

After your baby's umbilical cord is cut after birth, it's about 1–2 inches long. A plastic clamp is put on the cord before it's cut. The clamp is usually taken off before you leave the hospital. If you go home with the clamp still on, go back to the hospital and have a doctor or nurse take it off. Or let your baby's doctor take it off at the clinic. As the cord dries, it gets harder and shorter and turns black. It usually falls off between 1 and 2 weeks after birth.

Cord care is done to keep the area clean and to prevent infection. Sometimes drying agents (like alcohol) or home remedies are used for cord care. Most are not needed and some may be dangerous. If your family has a traditional cord-care method, talk with your baby's doctor about what you plan to do. Find out if your method is safe and if it really works.

How do you take care of the cord?

- Wash your hands well before cleaning the cord.
- Clean the cord daily or whenever it gets dirty from bowel movements. Use water or mild soap and water.
- Allow the cord to air-dry. Or dry it well using a cotton ball or swab. To promote drying, keep the diaper below the bellybutton area until the cord falls off.
- Call the doctor if the cord smells bad, if your baby's skin is red, or if you see pus or bright red blood. (It's normal to see a little dark red blood or clear yellow fluid as the cord falls off.)

Dressing Your Baby

You may be surprised that your baby needs so many clothes. Babies are messy. Your baby will probably spit up a little milk after he feeds. Also, pee and poop may leak out of his diaper. Sometimes he'll pee all over his clothes—and you—when his diaper is off. Try to have enough clothes so you have to wash his clothes only every few days.

Never leave your baby alone when changing his clothes or diaper. He may fall off the changing table, counter, or bed. Before you start to dress him, have all his clothes nearby so you won't need to reach and risk taking your hand off him. Some changing tables and pads have straps to hold the baby. However, older babies may be able to wiggle out of them.

Playing with Your Baby

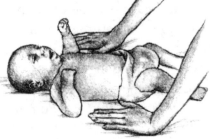

It's fun to play with your baby. Also, play is the way your baby learns about herself and the world around her. At first, play includes activities such as singing or talking to your baby. You may want to dance with her. She may enjoy being stroked or having a massage. Playing games such as peekaboo is fun for both of you. When your baby gets a little older, she'll enjoy rattles, books, and simple toys. Play with her when she's awake, alert, and calm.

Supplies for Baby Care

What do you need for your newborn baby? Here are a few suggestions:

Bed
- Crib or *bassinet* (baby bed), or have your baby in your bed
- 2–3 sheets for crib or bed
- 3–6 large, soft cotton blankets
- 1–2 blanket sleepers or warm blankets

Bath

- 1–2 baby towels or soft towels
- 2–3 baby washcloths
- Baby soap and shampoo
- Cotton swabs for umbilical cord
- Baby bathtub if desired

Diapers

- 4 dozen cloth diapers or disposable diapers (or diaper service if desired)
- 5–6 waterproof pants or wraps
- 6–8 thin washcloths or a box of diaper wipes
- Changing table if desired

Baby Clothes

- 4–6 undershirts or "onesies"
- 4–6 outfits and/or gowns
- 2–4 pairs of socks or booties
- Hat and warm sweater or jacket during the cold months

Travel

- Car seat (You must have one to take your baby home in a car.)
- Diaper bag or very large purse

Other Equipment (If Needed or Desired)

- Thermometer (digital or glass with a rounded tip and a red line, not a silver line) for taking your baby's temperature
- Front pack or sling to help you hold your baby
- Stroller
- Large exercise ball for bouncing your baby
- Baby swing

Keeping Your Baby Healthy and Safe

You can help protect your new baby from getting sick by washing your hands before you care for him. It gets rid of most germs. Also, ask your friends and family members to wash their hands before holding or touching your baby.

Health Care for Your Baby

Right after birth, the medical staff at the hospital will check your baby. Your baby's doctor may also examine him at the hospital before you go home.

The hospital staff performs certain screening tests to see if your baby is healthy. The March of Dimes suggests that all newborns have blood tests for at least 9 inherited diseases. They also advise hospitals to test new babies for hearing loss. Ask the hospital staff or your caregiver how many newborn screening tests are usually done at your hospital. (You can find out the tests done in your state by going to the March of Dimes website at www.marchofdimes.com.)

If you have a baby boy, you'll be asked about *circumcision* (removal of the skin at the end of the penis). If you choose to have him circumcised, it's usually done before he leaves the hospital. Or your doctor or your baby's doctor may do the procedure at the clinic or back at the hospital during the first week after birth. Circumcision isn't usually covered by insurance, so you'll probably have to pay for it yourself. Not as many boys are circumcised now as they were in the past. Talk to your baby's healthcare provider about your decision on circumcision.

Most families choose their baby's healthcare provider before birth. This may be a pediatrician, a family doctor, or a clinic with doctors and nurse practitioners. The person you choose depends on where you live and the kind of care you want. Your choice also depends on the type of healthcare coverage you have. If you don't have medical insurance, talk to your caregiver or clinic nurse to find out how to get free or low-cost medical care. Or call the Children's Health Care Hotline at 800-562-3022.

It's nice to talk to your baby's healthcare provider before the birth. You can talk about your choices for newborn care in the hospital. You can also plan your baby's first visit after the birth. Your baby needs to have a checkup when he's 3–10 days old. He'll be weighed to see if he's getting enough to eat. He'll also be checked for *jaundice* (yellow skin color that comes from too much bilirubin in the blood).

During his first year, your baby will be seen on a regular schedule to check on his growth and health. Your baby's healthcare provider will let you know when you'll need to make appointments. At all visits, ask questions about any concerns you may have about your baby.

✻ Tanya's Story ✻

After Michael was born, my best friend wanted to come see him and bring Lauren, her little girl, to play with Molly. As we talked, she told me that Lauren missed school all week with a cold and sore throat. I got nervous because I didn't want Michael or Molly to catch something. My friend said Lauren wasn't spreading germs anymore. But I told her I wanted her to wait a week. She told me I was being overprotective. Maybe I was, but I didn't want my kids getting sick. I was still tired and Michael was so young. She was a little mad at me, but she got over it. You have to look out for your kids' health, even if it's hard sometimes.

Immunizations

Your baby needs *immunizations* (shots or *vaccines*) to protect her from serious infections. In the United States, most families are not exposed to most of the diseases that require immunizations. However, these harmful germs are still around and can cause serious problems for your baby. You'll need a record of your child's shots when you take her to daycare or preschool. They don't want an outbreak of a disease such as chicken pox, measles, mumps, or polio.

Immunization shots are given at several times during your baby's first years. If possible, the vaccines are mixed together so only 1 shot is given at each age. Some vaccines need to be given 3 times in the first year. Then *booster shots* (repeat doses) are given at specific ages as your child grows older. Your baby's healthcare provider will tell you when the shots are needed for your baby.

Immunizations Are Important

Vaccine shots keep your baby healthy. They help prevent diseases that could seriously harm you or your baby.

Many babies are fussy for a few hours or days after a vaccine shot. It's normal for the injection site to be sore and tender. Some babies have a low fever. These reactions are fairly common.

Make sure to tell your healthcare provider if your baby has a more serious reaction. If you can't reach your doctor or clinic, take your baby to an urgent care clinic or the emergency room. These serious reactions aren't common, but they might be harmful:

- High fever
- Crying that lasts more than 3 hours
- Severe rash or redness
- *Seizure* (a fit or convulsion)

Taking Your Baby's Temperature

To quickly find out if your baby has a fever, put your hand on your baby's chest. Then touch the back of your neck. If your baby feels hotter than your neck, he may have a fever.

You can take your baby's temperature by putting a thermometer under his arm (*axillary* temperature) or in his bottom (*rectal* temperature). Check with your baby's healthcare provider to see what's recommended. Do **not** put a thermometer in your baby's mouth. (Use an oral thermometer only for a child older than 5 years.)

It's a good idea to use a digital thermometer because they're safer for babies. They can't break. If you use a glass thermometer, use one that has a rounded bulb end. If you have an old glass thermometer with a silver line, it contains mercury (a poison). Call your caregiver to learn the best way to get rid of it. Newer glass thermometers don't have mercury in them anymore. Ear thermometers aren't accurate for babies younger than 6 months old.

Many caregivers suggest that new parents take an underarm temperature. It helps to know that a normal body temperature is different depending on the area of the body used.

- A normal underarm temperature is about 97.6°F.
- A normal rectal temperature is about 99.6°F.
- A normal *oral* temperature (taken in the mouth) is about 98.6°F.

How to Use Your Thermometer

A digital thermometer simply needs to be turned on before using it. To clean it, follow the directions for your thermometer. With some brands, a plastic cover keeps it clean. With others, you wash it off after using it.

Before using a glass thermometer, hold it by the clear end (not the bulb end) at eye level and slowly turn it until you can see the red line. If the line is above 96°F, shake the thermometer until the line drops below 96°F. After using it, clean it with soap and warm water. Or you can you wipe it with a cotton ball that's been dipped in rubbing alcohol.

How to Take Your Baby's Temperature

To take an underarm temperature, put the thermometer in your baby's armpit. Bring his arm down and hold it against his body. Wait until the digital thermometer beeps and then read it. For a glass thermometer, wait 5 minutes. Then remove it and read the number where the red line stops.

To take a rectal temperature, lubricate the rounded tip of the thermometer (or the plastic cover) with petroleum jelly (like Vaseline). Put your baby on his back. Hold his ankles in 1 hand and bend his knees toward his chest. Gently insert the rounded end into his rectum until the bulb can't be seen (about ½ inch). Wait until the digital thermometer beeps, then take it out and read it. For a glass thermometer, hold it in place for about 3 minutes. Remove it and read the number where the red line stops.

When to Call for Medical Help

If you're worried about your baby's health, call her doctor or health clinic. You don't have to wait until your baby is seriously sick. You can call whenever you have questions about your baby's health.

When you call, here are some things the doctor or nurse may ask:

- What's your baby's temperature? (Take it before you call.)

- What symptoms do you notice? Is your baby coughing? Is she vomiting? Is there a rash?

- Is your baby fussier than usual? Is she acting differently than the way she usually acts? Is she very sleepy or floppy when awake?

- Is your baby eating normally? Are her bowel movements the same as usual?

- What have you done to treat the illness or condition? How did it work?

- Is anyone else sick at home or daycare?

- What's the name and phone number of your pharmacy or drugstore?

Have a paper and pencil handy to write down the healthcare provider's suggestions.

Newborn Warning Signs

If you notice any of these signs in the first month, call your baby's healthcare provider:

- *Fever.* Call if your baby's underarm temperature is above 99.5°F or her rectal temperature is above 100.4°F.

- *Yellowish color to your baby's face, chest, and the white parts of her eyes.* She may have jaundice.

- *Bright red bleeding or foul-smelling pus* appears at the cord or circumcision site.

- *Problems with feeding.* Call if your newborn baby eats fewer than 8 times in 24 hours or has trouble waking up for feedings.

- *Problems with bowel movements.* In the first week, call if there are no poopy diapers in a 24-hour period. Later, call if there are big changes in the number or type of BMs.

- *Not enough wet diapers.* Call if there are fewer than 6 wet diapers on the fourth day after birth (or each day after your breast milk comes in). With disposable diapers, put a small piece of paper towel in the diaper to find out when it gets wet.

- *Problems with breathing.* Call if your baby has blue lips or is struggling to breathe.

- *Call if anything about your baby causes you to be worried or concerned.*

Car Safety

Babies and children need to be in car seats when riding in a car. It's the law in the United States. A car seat can save your baby's life if it's put in correctly and used every time your baby rides in the car.

Here are some suggestions for keeping your baby safe in a car seat:

- Properly fasten the seat into your car. Read the directions for both the car seat and the car you'll be using. Some hospitals offer free car seat safety checks to make sure you've installed your car seat correctly.

- Use the right size and type of car seat. Newborn babies are placed in rear-facing car seats only. When your baby is over 20 pounds and is at least 1 year old, he can face forward.

- Put the car seat in the back seat. If you have a middle seat, use it. Keep your baby away from car windows and air bags.

- The car seat harness should be snug over your baby's shoulders. The harness retainer clip should be at the same level as your baby's armpits.

- Avoid wrapping your baby in blankets that pad his shoulders. Put him in the car seat and then put a blanket over him. Or use a warm outfit with arms and legs.

- Be careful about adding car seat pads. These can make your car seat unsafe. Instead, use a rolled-up towel or small blanket tucked in around your baby's head for support.

Safety at Home

In the first few months after birth, here are some ways to protect your baby:

- Keep your baby away from *secondhand smoke* (smoke from a cigarette or cigar). Babies who are exposed to secondhand smoke have more colds and ear infections. And they're at increased risk of SIDS.

- Have a safe place for your baby to sleep (either in your bed, a crib, or a bassinet). Have a firm mattress. If you're using a very old crib, make sure the bars are close enough together (at least 2⅜ inches apart) so she can't get her head through them.

- Keep at least 1 hand on your baby when she's on a changing table, bed, or other high surface. An active baby could fall off even before she's able to roll over.

- Watch your baby when young children are around. Most little kids don't know what's dangerous for a new baby. A toddler might think he's helping you by picking her up when she's crying. A child older than 10 years usually knows what's safe.

- Don't play roughly with your baby. Be gentle. Never throw her up in the air. And never shake her.

- Babies need good head support in the first months. Even when your baby can hold her head up well, she still needs to be handled gently.

- Don't have strings or cords near your baby. She could wrap them around her neck and choke. Avoid strings on her clothing, near her crib, and attached to her pacifier.

As your baby grows and becomes more active, she needs your help to stay safe. Babies who crawl and climb are more likely to get hurt. When your baby is about 4–6 months old, you should start babyproofing your home.

❧ Cami's Story ❧

Don't learn about baby safety the hard way, like I did. I thought Tommy couldn't roll over. He was only 3 months old. Anyway, I left him on the bed while I went to the bathroom. Then the phone rang and he started to cry. I talked for a few minutes and then I heard a CLUNK! I yelled, "Oh, my gosh!" and ran into the room. There he was on the floor beside the bed. Luckily, he was okay—just a bump on the head, and a good scare for me. He must have worked his way off the bed while he was crying. I felt so guilty. I haven't done anything like that since. We were lucky once, but I learned my lesson. I still feel bad every time I think about it.

A Note to Families Having Another Baby

Older children may or may not be excited about having a new baby. Even if they're excited before the baby comes, that can change once the baby is in your home night and day. One thing is certain: Life is never the same for the older child or for you after the birth of a new baby.

Your older child's behavior may surprise and disappoint you during the first weeks after your baby's birth. Your child may react in a variety of ways:

- He may go back to wanting to breastfeed or take a bottle, sucking his thumb, or wetting his pants.

- He may throw temper tantrums.

- He may be angry with you or the baby.

- He may not pay attention to the baby, or he may ignore you.

- His sleeping and eating habits may change.

- He may be nice and helpful with the baby.

What can you do to help your older child adjust?

- Prepare your child before the baby's born. Tell him about babies. Read books about being an older brother or sister. Talk with him and find out what he knows about babies and being an older sibling.

- Try to accept your child's reactions as normal responses to stress. Don't let your child harm himself or the baby, but understand his feelings.

- Plan some time alone with your older child.

- Show him photos of you caring for him as a baby.

- Let him help you with baby care, if he wants. Be sure to stay with your children when they're together.

- When visitors bring gifts for the baby, let your older child open them. You may encourage visitors to bring a gift for your older child, too.

✷ Tanya's Story ✷

Taking care of our baby was *so* much easier the second time. I knew how to change diapers, give him a bath, and soothe him when he cried. So, I didn't worry as much. After a while, Molly started paying attention to Michael. She sang and danced for him. She even nursed her doll while I was breastfeeding. That was fun to see. I was glad when she started enjoying her baby brother. It felt like we were finally becoming a family!

A Note to Fathers

When your baby first comes home, it may seem like the baby's mother is better at taking care of the baby than you. If your baby is breastfed, you may feel like there's nothing you can do. You'll be surprised at how much fathers and partners can do!

You can:

- Help feed your baby by making sure your baby's mother eats well every day. This helps her make breast milk for your baby.

- Bathe the baby. This can be a special time for you and your baby. You might try taking your baby into the tub or shower with you. Be careful, though, as babies are slippery when wet.

- Relax while your baby takes a nap with you. Lean back with your baby lying on your chest. You'll both love it.

- Dance or walk with your baby. Sway to the music. Sing to her. She knows your voice and feels safe in your arms.

- Rock in a rocking chair or gently bounce on a big exercise ball. Babies love movement.

- Take your baby for a stroller ride. Getting out of the house can be good for the whole family.

You're an important part of your child's life. By being with your baby in the first weeks and months, you'll get to know each other. You'll be amazed at how deeply and quickly you fall in love with your new baby.

Help and Resources for You and Your Baby

This list provides information about organizations, groups, agencies, and services that might be helpful during pregnancy and after having your baby. Your caregivers may also help you find resources in your area.

Pregnancy Health and Safety Resources

Centers for Disease Control and Prevention

Their Tobacco Information and Prevention Source (TIPS) website can help you stop smoking.

www.cdc.gov/tobacco/how2quit.htm

March of Dimes

This group provides information and support about having a safe pregnancy and healthy baby. Contact them to find out the newborn screening tests done in your state.

www.marchofdimes.com/pnhec/298_834.asp

Maternity Wise

This organization offers information to help women make informed choices about pregnancy and birth.

www.maternitywise.org

212-777-5000

National Domestic Violence Hotline

This organization helps victims of abuse and violence. Contact them if you need suggestions on how to handle a bad relationship.

www.ndvh.org

800-799-7233

Maternity Care Resources

American College of Obstetricians and Gynecologists

This organization has the names of obstetricians in your state. Also, most hospitals have a list of doctors who deliver babies.

www.acog.org   (Click on "Find an Ob-Gyn.")

202-638-5577

American College of Nurse-Midwives

This organization can help you find a
certified nurse-midwife (CNM) in your area.

www.midwife.org/find

240-485-1800

Midwives Alliance of North America

This organization has the names of licensed midwives (LM).
Contact them to ask for ones in your area.

membership@mana.org/memberlist.html

888-923-MANA (888-923-6262)

National Association of Childbearing Centers

This association can help you find a birth center in your area.

www.birthcenters.org/fabc/index.php

Low-Cost Care Resources

Child Welfare League of America

This organization has information about low-cost medical care. Medicaid
funds are available for pregnant women and children younger than 6 years
old whose family income is less than a certain amount. Contact them to find
the phone numbers for Medicaid agencies in your state. Your state agency
can tell you whether you qualify for medical assistance.

www.cwla.org/programs/health/healthstate.htm

877-KIDS-NOW (877-543-7669)

Women, Infants, and Children (WIC)

The WIC program offers food for pregnant women and breastfeeding help
for new mothers whose income is less than a certain amount. They can help
you find parenting help and support. Also, your caregiver may help you find
your local WIC office.

www.fns.usda.gov/wic

Childbirth Classes and Birth Partner Resources

Doulas of North America (DONA)

This organization can help you find a doula
(a professional birth partner) in your area.

www.dona.org/FindingADoula.html

888-788-DONA (888-788-3662)

Great Starts Birth & Family Education

This non-profit organization sells this book and offers classes and support for new families in and around Seattle, Washington.

www.greatstarts.org

206-789-0883

International Childbirth Education Association

This association provides information about finding a childbirth educator in your area. You could also call your local hospital to learn about childbirth classes near you.

www.icea.org/us1.htm

952-854-8660

Lamaze International

This organization provides information about how to find a Lamaze childbirth class near you.

www.lamaze.org/expectant/FindLamaze.asp

Baby Care Resources

American Academy of Pediatrics

This organization offers information about keeping your child healthy, parenting, and finding a pediatrician (doctor for babies and children).

www.aap.org

Consumer Product Safety Commission

This agency offers information about home safety and unsafe baby care products.

www.cpsc.gov

301-504-7923

Immunization Action Coalition

This organization offers information about shots to keep your baby healthy.

www.immunize.org

651-647-9009
(Hotline for questions about shots: 800-232-2522)

National Highway Traffic Safety Administration (NHTSA)

Their Child Passenger Safety (CPS) department offers information about infant and child car seats.

www.nhtsa.gov/CPS

SIDS Alliance

This organization provides information about SIDS and other causes of infant death. They offer suggestions about safe sleeping.

www.sidsalliance.org

800-221-7437

American SIDS Institute

This organization provides information about ways to reduce the risk of SIDS.

www.sids.org/nprevent.htm

800-232-SIDS (800-232-7437)

Breastfeeding Resources

International Lactation Consultant Association (ILCA)

This association keeps records of breastfeeding professionals who are International Board Certified Lactation Consultants (IBCLCs). Contact them to find a breastfeeding expert in your area.

gotwww.net/ilca

919-861-5577

La Leche League (LLL)

This organization offers mother-baby groups for breastfeeding support. Contact them to find a LLL group near you. Or ask them to help you find breastfeeding consultants in your area.

www.lalecheleague.org/WebIndex.html

847-519-7730

National Women's Health Information Center

This agency answers breastfeeding questions.

www.4woman.gov/breastfeeding

800-944-9662

Parenting Resources

County Public Health Department or State Health Department

These departments can give you information about agencies that offer help with parenting issues. Contact the health department for your state, county, or city to learn more about parenting resources near you.

National Healthy Mothers, Healthy Babies Coalition

This organization offers help with breastfeeding and parenting.

www.hmhb.org/family.html

703-836-6110

National Organization of Mothers of Twins Clubs, Inc. (NOMOTC)

This organization provides information and support for families having more than one baby. Contact them to learn the names of local parents of multiples groups.

www.nomotc.org/welcome/zipsearch.htm

877-540-2200

Parents Without Partners

This organization provides information and support for single parents and their children. Contact them to find a group in your area.

www.parentswithoutpartners.org/chapterfind.asp

561-391-8833

Planned Parenthood

This organization can tell you about methods you can use to avoid getting pregnant.

www.plannedparenthood.org/bc

800-230-PLAN (800-230-7526)

Your Local Community College

Many community colleges have classes for parents. Contact the family life education department at your local community college.

Postpartum Depression and Loss Resources

Depression After Delivery

This group is a resource for women with postpartum mood disorders. Contact them to find a support group in your area.

www.charityadvantage.com/depressionafterdelivery/supportgroups.asp

Postpartum Support International

This group offers help to women with postpartum mood disorders. Contact them to learn about a mothers' support group in your area.

www.postpartum.net

Share Pregnancy & Infant Loss Support, Inc.

This group offers support for families who have lost a baby by early pregnancy loss, stillbirth, or newborn death.

www.nationalshareoffice.com

800-821-6819

Index

Centers for Disease Control and Prevention, 251
Certified nurse-midwives (CNMs), 23
Cervix, **3**
    during active labor, 149
    changes in, 76–77
    dilation of, 78
    in early phase of labor, 86, 87
    effacement of, 77
    ripening of, 77
    during transition phase of labor, 96
Cesarean birth, **152**
    for breech babies, 80
    first hours after, 160
    home after, 164
    pain relief after, 161–62
    placenta and, 32
    procedure of, 156–58
    reasons for having, 153–55
    recovery from, 162–63
    risks associated with, 156
Cheeses, 39
Chemicals, harmful, 52
Childbirth
    birth plan on, 63–67
    choices on, 61
    classes on, 62
    length of, 75
    packing bags prior to, 70–71
    place of, 23–24
    registering at hospital for, 69
    touring hospital prior to, 68
    See also Birth; Cesarean birth; Labor
Child Welfare League of America, 252
Cigarette smoking, 50
Circumcision, **238**
Cloth diapers, 233
Clothing, baby, 235–36, 237
Cocaine, 51
Colds, home remedies for, 49
Colostrum, **170**, 191
Comfort measures
    for active labor phase, 90

for early labor phase, 87
for labor pain, 116, 120
Conception, 1–2
Constipation, **8**, 56, 172
Contraception, 187
Contractions
    active labor phase, 89
    after birth, 104
    breathing patterns during, 116
    checking for, 28
    early phase of labor, 86, 87, 94
    with long and slow labor, 147, 148–49
    non-labor, 9
    with Pitocin, 143
    preterm labor, **11**, 27, 28, 29
    progression of, 82
    rests in, 75
    second stage of labor, 98
    timing labor, 79–80
Coos, **222**
Coping skills
    attention-focusing methods, 124–25
    breathing patterns, 115–18
    relaxation, 109–15
Coping well during labor, **109**
Cough, home remedies for, 49
Crack, 51
Cramps, leg and foot, **58**–59
Crying
    as an infant cue, 222
    comforting baby for, 225–27
    excessive, 228
    responding to, 228
C-section. *See* Cesarean birth

D

Dairy products, 37, 38
Dehydration, **202**
Depression After Delivery, 255
Descent, **80**
"Development" period for baby, 7
Diabetes, **30**
Diapering, 232–34

formula for, 215
preparing formula for, 216
tips for, 217–18
Fourth stage (labor), **81**
Frequency, of contractions, **79**–80
Fruits, 37
Full-term babies, 76

G

Galactosemia, **215**
Gas pains, 163
Genital herpes infection, 153
German measles, 29
Gestational diabetes, **30**–31
Grains, 37
Great Starts Birth & Family
  Education, 253
Growth spurts, **198**

H

Hand expressing, **204**, 211, 212
Headache, home remedies for, 48
Head-lift exercise, 171
Head shape, baby's, 219
Health care. *See* Medical care;
  Prenatal care
Hearing, newborn's, 220
Heartburn, **55**
Heart disease, 153
Hemorrhoids, **11**, 56, 173
Herbal products, 39
High blood pressure, 31–32
High-needs baby, **224**
HIV positive, 153
Home birth, 71
Homes remedies, 48, 49
Hormones, **2**–3, 76
Hospital
  choosing, 23
  packing for, 70–71
  registering at, 69
  returning home from, 165
  tests and procedures for
    unborn baby in, 91–92

touring, 68
Hot tubs, 53
Hunger cues, **197**
Hypertension, **31**
Hypoallergenic formula, **215**

I

Immunization Action Coalition, 253
Immunizations, **240**–41
Inducing labor, **139**
Induction, **139**
Infant cues, **222**
Infections, 29–30
Informed consent, **69**
Injection, **132**
Intensity, of contractions, **79**, 80
Internal electronic fetal monitoring, **92**
Internal pressure balance, **129**
International Childbirth Education
  Association, 253
International Lactation Consultant
  Association (ILCA), 203, 254
Intravenous (IV) fluids, **93**, 150
Iron-fortified formula, **215**

J

Jaundice, **202**, 239

K

Kegel exercises, **43**, 168, 173

L

Labor, **75**
  birth partner's role in, 121–22
  cervical changes during, 76–78
  contacting caregiver before, 85
  fetal monitoring of baby
    during, 91–92
  first stage of, 86–96
  inducing, 139
  intravenous fluid intake
    during, 93
  long and slow, 147–52
  position for pushing during, 100

possible signs of, 83–84
second stage of, 98–101
short and fast, 144–47
stages of, 81
starting, methods for, 140–43
start of, 76
third stage of, 102–3
urge to push during, 98–99
See also Labor pain
Labor pain
baths/showers for, 126
breathing patterns for, 115–18
causes of, 107
circumstances influencing
extent of, 107–8
comfort measures for, 120
coping with back pain and,
128–30
focusing attention for, 124–25
helpful hints on handling, 138
massage and touch for, 125
medicines used for, 131–36
positions and movements for,
127
reducing pain medicine for,
137–38
relaxation for, 109–15
warm/cold packs for, 126
Lactation, **192**
Lactation consultants, 203
La Leche League (LLL), 203, 254
Lamaze International, 253
Latching, **195**
helping baby with, 195–96
sore nipples and, 209
Legs
shaking, 105
swollen, 58
Length, of contractions, **79**
Light breathing, 117–18
Lightening, **11**
Linea nigra, **8**
Liquid concentrate formula, **216**
Local anesthesia, **131**, 136
Lochia, **104**, 166–67

Long labor, 147–52
Low-impact exercise, **41**
Low-risk pregnancy, **24**

M

March of Dimes, 251
Marijuana, 51
Mask of pregnancy, **8**
Massage, 125
Mastitis, **206**
Maternity Wise, 251
Meconium, **232**
Medical care/procedures
for baby, 238–40
in birth plan, 66
birth without, 145–47
for long and early labor,
148–49
postpartum, 175
for pushing baby out, 151–52
for slow active labor, 150–51
Medicine
birth control, 187
taking, during pregnancy,
47–49
See also Pain medicine
Membranes, **3**
Menstrual periods, 167
Methamphetamines, 51–52
Midwives, **23**
See also Caregiver
Midwives Alliance of North
America, 252
Miscarriage, **52**
Morning sickness, **6**, 54
Motion (movement)
baby's enjoyment of, 221
calming baby with, **226**
for labor pain, 127
Mucous plug, **3**
Multiple pregnancy, **16**
Muscle cramps, 58–59
Muscle tension, **44**

N

Narcotics, **131**, 132, 161
National Association of
   Childbearing Centers, 252
National Domestic Violence
   Hotline, 251
National Healthy Mothers, Healthy
   Babies Coalition, 203, 254
National Highway Traffic Safety
   Administration (NHTSA), 253
National Organization of Mothers of
   Twins Club, Inc. (NOMOTC), 255
National Women's Health Center, 254
Natural childbirth, **65**, 131
Naturopaths, **23**
Nausea, drugs to treat, 49
   See also Morning sickness
Nesting urge, **83**
Nipples
   avoiding sore, 209
   flat, 204
Nipple stimulation, **141**
Non-food substances, 39
Non-stress test, **25**
Nurse practitioners, **23**
Nursing, **192**
   See also Breastfeeding
Nutrients, 36

O

Obstetrician, **16**, **23**
   See also Caregiver
Older child
   adapting to new baby, 248–49
   pregnancy with, 14–15
Oral temperature, **241**
Out-of-hospital birth, 23–24
Ovaries, **1**, 191
Oxytocin, **141**

P

Pain
   afterpains, after childbirth, 167
   in birth canal, following birth,
      168–69

breast, 170
   following cesarean birth, 161–62
   muscle and joint, 172
   sore nipples, 209
   See also Contractions; Labor pain
Pain medicine.
   in birth plan, 64–65
   cesarean birth and, 161
   deciding to use, 131
   local anesthesia, 136
   narcotics, 132
   reducing amount of, 137–38
   See also Epidural
Pain relief, in birth plan, 65–66
Pain relievers, 48
Parenting
   receiving outside help for, 189–90
   resources on, 254–55
   trial-and-error method of, 224
Parents Without Partners, 255
Partner
   early caring for newborn by, 190
   helping with the baby at home,
      249–50
   during labor, 90
   relaxation with, 113
   worries of, 19–20
   See also Birth partner
Pasteurized cheese, **39**
Patient-controlled analgesia
   (PCA), **161**
Pelvic floor muscles, exercising, 43
Pelvic tilt exercise, 57
Peri bottle, **168**
Perineum, **99**
Personality, baby's, 224
Physical changes
   first trimester, 6
   in partners, 20
   during postpartum, 166–73
   second trimester, 8–9
   third trimester, 11
Pica, **39**
Piles, **173**
Pitocin, **135**, 142

Rotation, **80**
Routines, **68**, 91

S

Saunas, 53
Sea-Bands, 54
Seat belts, 47
Secondhand smoke, 246
Second stage (labor), **81**, 98–101
    long, 151–52
Second trimester
    baby's development during, 7
    changes in mother during, 8
Secretions, **186**
Seizure, **241**
Semi-sitting, **100**
Sexual intercourse
    after childbirth, 167, 186–87
    during pregnancy, 13–14
    starting labor with, 141
Share Pregnancy and Infant Loss
  Support, Inc., 255
Showers, 126
Siblings, 248–49
Side effects
    cesarean birth, 156
    of epidurals, 134
    of local anesthesia, 136
    of narcotics, 132
SIDS Alliance, 254
Single women
    giving baby up for adoption, 18
    pregnancy for, 17–18
Sitz bath, **169**
Sleep (baby), 229, 231
Sleep (mother)
    during postpartum, 178–79
    prenatal, 44, 60
Slow breathing, 116–17
Smell, baby's sense of, **221**
Smiling, newborn baby's, 223
Smoking, 50
Solid foods, **191**
Sperm cells, **1**–2
Spermicidal, **187**

Spine, **133**
Sports, 41–42
State-licensed midwives (LMs), 23
Sterilizing (bottle), **217**
Stitches, 168
Stools, **232**
Street drugs, 51
Stress, 44, 45, 46
Stretch marks, **11**
Sudden Infant Death Syndrome
  (SIDS), **230**, 231
Supplements, **39**
Support system
    for breastfeeding help, 203, 214
    building, 46
    examples of helpful people in, 17
    new mother's support groups, 185
    during postpartum, 176–77
    receiving help from, 47
Swaddling, **221**, 226
Swelling, ankle/leg, 58
Symptoms
    of infections, 30
    of labor, 83
    of pregnancy-induced
      hypertension, 31–32
    of preterm labor, 27–28

T

Taste, baby's sense of, **221**
Temperature, taking baby's, 241–42
Testicles, **1**
Tests
    Apgar test, for baby, 103
    fetal monitoring of baby, 91–92
    on mother, during labor, 93
    prenatal, 24–25
Third stage (labor), **81**, 102–3
Third trimester
    baby's development during, 10
    emotions during, 12
    physical changes during, 11
Tobacco, 50
Touch, baby's sense of, **221**
Touch relaxation, **113**, 125

Toxins, 52
Toxoplasmosis, **53**
Transition, **86**
Trial-and-error method of
 parenting, **224**
Trimesters, **5**
Triplets, 16
Twins, 16
Tylenol, 48

U

Ultrasound scan, **25**
Umbilical cord, **3**, 235
Underarm temperature, **242**
Urethra, **43**
Urge to push, **98**–99
Urination
 after cesarean birth, 163
 after childbirth, 172
Urine, **3**
Uterus, **3**
 after birth, 105
 during postpartum, 166–67
 strength of, 75

V

Vaccines, **230**, 240
Vacuum extractor, **152**
Vagina, **3**
Vaginal birth after cesarean
 (VBAC), **155**
Vaginal bleeding. *See* Lochia
Vaginal dryness, 186
Vascular spiders, **11**
Vegetables, 37
Vernix, **102**, 219
Vision, newborn's, 220
Vitamins, prenatal, 181
Vomiting, drugs to treat, 49
 See also Morning sickness

W

Walking
 after cesarean birth, 163
 starting labor with, 140

Warning signs
 for newborn, 244
 during post partum, 174
 of pregnancy problems, 26
Water, giving baby, 202
Weight gain (baby), 200
Weight gain (mother), 9, 40
Weight loss (mother), 181
Witch hazel, **169**
Womb, **3**
Women, Infants, and Children
 (WIC) program, 38, 203, 252
Wristbands, 54

Z

Zinc oxide, **234**

Also from Meadowbrook Press

100,000 Baby Names
This is the #1 baby name book, and is the most complete guide for helping you name your baby. It contains over 100,000 popular and unusual names from around the world, complete with origins, meanings, variations, and famous namesakes. It also includes the most recently available top 100 names for girls and boys, as well as over 300 helpful lists of names to consider and avoid.

Pregnancy, Childbirth, and the Newborn
More complete and up-to-date than any other pregnancy guide, this remarkable book is the "bible" for childbirth educators. It includes a thorough treatment of pregnancy tests, complications, infections, and medications and detailed advice on creating a birth plan.

The Official Lamaze® Guide: Giving Birth with Confidence
Finally, a book that tells you what to expect, not what to fear, during pregnancy and birth! In it, leading childbirth educators Lothian and DeVries show pregnant women how to have confidence in their ability to give birth naturally. It provides expectant couples with detailed information on how to handle whatever issues arise.

Baby & Child Emergency First Aid
Edited by Mitchell J. Einzig, MD. This user-friendly book is the next best thing to 911, with a quick-reference index, large illustrations, and easy-to-read instructions on handling the most common childhood emergencies.

First-Year Baby Care
This is one of the leading baby-care books to guide you through your baby's first year. It contains complete information on the basics of baby care, including bathing, diapering, medical facts, and feeding your baby.

Feed Me! I'm Yours
Parents love this easy-to-use, economical guide to making baby food at home. More than 200 recipes cover everything a parent needs to know about teething foods, nutritious snacks, and quick, pleasing lunches. Now recently revised.

**We offer many more titles written to delight, inform, and entertain.
To order books with a credit card or browse our full
selection of titles, visit our website at:**

www.meadowbrookpress.com

or call toll free to place an order, request a free catalog, or ask a question:

1-800-338-2232

Meadowbrook Press • 5451 Smetana Drive • Minnetonka, MN • 55343